OUT OF THE MOUTH OF BABE

Curated by **Kelly Bennett**
with **Brent Stevens** and **Stu Dressler**

For Curtis: "manager," coach, and #1 fan, always and all ways.
—Kelly Bennett

I thank the Ruth Stevens Family—Brent, Tom, Anita, and Julia—for bringing me into the world of Babe Ruth nearly twenty years ago. Not only have I had the privilege of an inside look at Babe, his life, and his on-field accomplishments, but I have also been rewarded with the family's friendship, which I value greatly.
—Stu Dressler

I want to thank all of my family for their love and support in my endeavors.
—Brent Stevens

Text copyright © 2025 by Kelly Bennett with Brent Stevens and Stu Dressler
All rights reserved.

Published by Familius LLC, www.familius.com
PO Box 1130, Sanger, CA 93657

Familius books are available at special discounts for bulk purchases, whether for sales promotions or for family or corporate use. For more information, contact Familius Sales at orders@familius.com.

Library of Congress Control Number: 2024945955

Print ISBN 2024945955
Ebook ISBN 9798893965018

Printed in China

Edited by Peg Sandkam, and <proofreader's name>
Cover and book design by Carlos Mireles-Guerrero

10 9 8 7 6 5 4 3 2 1

First Edition

Old-Timers' All-Star Game, August 26, 1943. The game raised more than 800 million dollars in war bonds. Along with Babe, Honus Wagner, Walter Johnson, Connie Mack, Tris Speaker, Lefty Grove, Eddie Collins, Al Simmons, George Dickey, George Sisler, and Home Run Baker took the field. Babe hit his final home run ever in that game.

FOREWORD BY TOM STEVENS

Even though he passed away more than seventy-five years ago, public fascination with Babe Ruth is as great today as it has ever been, to the continuing wonder and amazement of our family. He still holds major league batting records that are virtually unassailable, and this includes modern-day computer-generated parameters, such as wins above replacement (WAR). When it comes to discussing baseball superlatives, his name is most often the first mentioned among sportswriters and announcers. His name is still recognized around the world today, even in countries that have no interest in baseball. At last count, there were over seventy books written about Babe Ruth, more than any other sports figure, save Jackie Robinson. Another book about Babe Ruth? Well, why not? The interest is certainly still there.

I was already familiar with Kelly's work, having read and thoroughly enjoyed *The House that Ruth Built*, which was written for young readers. So I was delighted when she asked me to review her newest book, *Out of the Mouth of Babe*.

Kelly has chosen a slightly unconventional format for her book, and for me, that is a large part of its appeal. Using the broadest of brush strokes, she has painted a thoroughly likable and affectionate portrait of the Babe that employs biographical text, supplemented by thoughtfully chosen photos and quotes. Many of the photos that have been included were selected from the Ruth family's collection and we are happy to share them with fans. The result is a true coffee table book in that you can open it to almost any random page and soon become engrossed.

As Babe Ruth's grandson, I have made it a point to try and read virtually everything ever written about him to see if I can learn anything new—in this regard, *Out of the Mouth of Babe* does not disappoint. For example, I was never aware that in 1921, he was offered a "home run incentive"—$50 for each home run that he hit—in addition to his playing contract.

The book begins with Babe's rough-and-tumble start in life, growing up in the heart of Baltimore's bowery and his neglected upbringing and subsequent internment at St Mary's Industrial school from the ages of seven to nineteen, where he was trained to be a tailor and learned to play baseball. It was here that he met "the greatest man he ever knew" in the person of Martin Leo Boutlier, also known as Brother Mathias, an Xaverian Brother who took him under his wing and played a positive role throughout his adult life as well, long after he left St Mary's. The story continues in Baltimore, where he had a short tenure as a pitcher for the Baltimore Orioles; it was here that George was given the nickname that would stay with him for the rest of his life. Then on to the Red Sox, where he established himself as the best left-handed pitcher in the American League. But there was something else, oh yes, he could also hit the ball harder and further, more often than any other player before or since. He was then sold to the Yankees, where over the next fourteen years, he established himself, according to Ted Williams, as the greatest hitter that baseball has ever seen. And along the way, Babe endeared himself to millions of fans, not only thrilling them with his baseball exploits and heroics, but charming them as well, just by being the Babe.

By all accounts, my grandfather was a lot of fun to be around, a barrel of monkeys and a big brass band all rolled into one. Whether eating hot dogs or signing baseballs, visiting kids in orphanages and hospitals, or making appearances for charity or to sell war bonds during World War II, the Babe was in a class by himself. A couple of years ago, I learned something I thought was extraordinary: Sometimes before a ballgame, he would buy the kids in the bleachers hot dogs and soda pop and then sit and visit with them. And he did this at away games, too, not just Yankee Stadium.

I would like to share yet another quote that I think personifies the essence of Babe Ruth. This comes from Red Sox pitcher Harry Hooper, one of Babe's earliest teammates. "Sometimes I still can't believe what I saw. This nineteen-year-old kid, crude, poorly educated, only lightly brushed by the social veneer we call civilization, gradually transformed into the idol of American youth and the symbol of baseball the world over—a man loved by more people and with an intensity of feeling that perhaps has never been equaled before or since."

Before she passed away, I asked my mother, Julia, what she would like people to know about her father after she was gone. She said, "make sure you tell them what a great guy he was." *Out of the Mouth of Babe* has done an admirable job.

INTRODUCTION BY MARTY APPEL

What an honor it is to be asked to contribute to a Babe Ruth book!

I mean, BABE RUTH!!! The name still evokes attention and awe, all these years later.

Me and the Babe, we go way back. I was born on August 7, 1948, and nine days later, eleven miles away, he passed away. I was just a babe, but he was The Babe. And I was told that when I heard the news, I cried like a baby.

I wasn't alone. The news accounts of the day confirm it. There was a line outside Yankee Stadium to view him in his casket that stretched halfway around the ballpark. Grandparents wanted to show their grandchildren his body so they could say "I saw Babe Ruth."

Here's the most remarkable thing about the enduring respect the nation has for the Babe: Name any major sport, ask about its greatest player ever, and the answer is likely to be someone from the television age who we saw up close in our lifetime. Wayne Gretzky, Muhammad Ali, Pele, Michael Jordan, Tiger Woods (or Jack Nicklaus), Serena Williams, Tom Brady (or Jim Brown), Caitlin Clark, or Roger Federer-Rafa Nadal-Novak Djokovic. And yet, more than a century after his arrival on the big stage of New York, in baseball, it remains Babe Ruth.

Babe Ruth played his last game some ninety years ago. People in his time, if not in person, mostly saw him on movie theater newsreels, always hitting a home run. Few if any people remain with any real mind image of him sliding into a base, catching a fly ball, or throwing out a runner. And yes, he did all those things well.

He was the third best-known person in America in his day—after the president and, I suppose, Charlie Chaplin. And his importance remains. American history books still include him, along with Jackie Robinson.

As historian John Thorn points out, if the Babe had lived into his seventies, (he was only fifty-three when he died), he would likely have been a frequent guest on Johnny Carson's *The Tonight Show*, and for many, that might have been the lasting image, with the big cigar and hardy laugh. He might have co-hosted the Macy's Thanksgiving Day Parade or done color commentary on the World Series.

And then there is Babe and William Shakespeare. The Babe and the Bard. In a sense, he is America's William Shakespeare. Name the greatest playwright ever and it still comes up Shakespeare, all these centuries later. America's greatest baseball player? Ruth. Is it a stretch to link the two? As usual, there is a perfect Shakespearean quote for Babe Ruth: Hamlet, speaking of his father said, "I shall not look upon his like again."

Ruth-signed baseballs go for thousands of dollars in the collectibles market today (in 2023, his signature on a National League baseball went for $137,620), and yet that fact remains an anomaly in the world of supply and demand. A joke in his time was that "there is nothing so rare as a baseball not signed by Babe Ruth." But indeed, there was no more generous signer than was Babe, and there are photos of him signing hundreds of balls at single sittings on behalf of a corporate sponsor ("Take a test drive, get a Babe Ruth signed ball!"). Whatever became of all those balls, I wonder.

I went to work in the Yankees PR department in 1968. I was nineteen, and it had been twenty years since that line wrapped around Yankee Stadium to view the Babe. To many who worked there, that might have felt like yesterday. His presence was always felt.

I got to know many people who worked with him or ran around with him, including our clubhouse man Pete Sheehy (who joined the Yankees in 1927) and my office mate in the original Stadium, Jackie Farrell. Jackie, an old *New York Daily News* boxing writer, was barely five feet tall. He was a great character in his own right and Babe loved him. He even called him "Jackie," not "kid." And thanks to Jackie's diminutive stature, he remembered his name. Jackie accompanied Babe on many personal appearances, as he would with Joe DiMaggio, Mickey Mantle, and Bobby Murcer in future years. Oh, the questions I would pour on Pete, Jackie, the aging John Drebinger of *The New York Times* (who said Babe never had an enemy; everyone just loved the big lug), or our coach Frankie Crosetti (a Babe teammate)—I couldn't get enough detail.

Then there was Little Ray Kelly, the Babe's mascot, with whom I had a friendship, and who lived until 2001. Little Ray (he insisted on being called Little) was the tyke from Riverside Drive whom Babe would drive to games, pose with for pictures, and occupy a spot in the dugout. He wasn't a batboy, just a mascot.

"Little Ray," I would say, "how did the other players feel about him having a mascot in the dugout just for himself?"

"Are you kidding?!" he would respond. "He was Babe Ruth. He could do whatever he wanted. He put a lot of money in those guy's pockets."

On Old-Timers' Day, I would make arrangements to have Claire Ruth, the Babe's widow—and later, daughter Julia Ruth Stevens and her family—as a special guest. Talk about baseball royalty.

Claire died just days after the 1976 World Series ended. Her funeral was the same day I was going to the Manhattan bank to cash in my unused Series tickets (it only went four games), so I attended the church service. I was with our outfielder Roy White, who was also returning tickets, and we wound up being asked to be honorary pall bearers. It was an honor that remains in my thoughts to this day.

I felt Babe's presence when we moved into the remodeled Stadium in 1976 and I had a large window in my office overlooking the field. (It was replicated on the Seinfeld sitcom as George Costanza's office.) Aided by that magnificent view, there was not a day in which I wasn't reminded that this was still "the house that Ruth built." I never got it out of my mind.

In 2008, I visited "old" Yankee Stadium with Tom Stevens. We wanted to talk to Lonn Trost, the team's Chief Operating Officer, about the "House that Ruth Built" nickname and how Babe would be remembered in the new one being built across 161st Street. Out of that visit came an invitation for Julia to throw out the first pitch at the final game of 2008 and for Babe Ruth Plaza to be so named at the new site in 2009.

And so more than a century after he first joined the Yankees, when he began out-homering even full teams in the rest of the league, through a time when interest in the game soared and he was on the tip of everyone's tongue with his diamond feats, the Babe abides.

RUTHIAN: RUTH-IAN/RUTH'-I-AN (ADJ.)

THE STATE OF BEING GREATER THAN THE BEST; MAJESTIC; DENOTING A SUPREME OR INSURMOUNTABLE LEVEL; SURPASSING ALL OTHERS.

CONTENTS

"YOU'VE GOT TO KEEP IN THERE SWINGING."

"Ruth has hit almost as many home runs as Heinz has pickles. In fact, he is a greater pickler than the world has ever before known."
—*The New York Times*, September 25, 1920

Signed photo of Babe during spring training with the NY Yankees, likely in St. Petersburg, Florida.

"I THANK HEAVEN WE HAVE HAD BASEBALL IN THIS WORLD . . . THE KIDS . . . OUR NATIONAL PASTIME."

"If Babe were alive today I get the feeling he'd still be a big fan favorite. He'd still love kids. He'd still love playing the game. He'd still get a thrill out of people asking for his autograph and he'd still take the time to give it to them."
—Greg Schwalenberg, curator of the Babe Ruth Birthplace Museum, as quoted in *The Babe Book* by Ernestine Miller

Babe signing baseballs for children in Vancouver, Canada, at the end of his 1926 Vaudeville tour.

"THE REAL TEST OF HITTING GREATNESS IS THE ABILITY TO STEP UP THERE AND HIT WHEN A HIT WILL MEAN A RUN."

"It wasn't just that he hit more home runs than anybody else, he hit them better, higher, farther, with more theatrical timing and a more flamboyant flourish. Nobody could strike out like Babe Ruth. Nobody circled the bases with the same pigeon-toed, mincing majesty."
—Red Smith, sportswriter

"Babe surely delivered with a home run." Babe, the Red Sox catcher, and umpire, looking toward the right-field stands at Fenway Park, circa 1933.

"MY IDEA OF A REAL BALL PLAYER IS THE FELLOW WHO CAN TAKE THE BAD BREAKS WITH A GRIN AND COME UP FIGHTING."

"Before radio, since major league baseball was not played west of the Mississippi, newspapers and magazines were the only way fans could see the Babe. Barnstorming was a win-win for all involved. Babe made good money because he got a percentage of the gate, and people got to see their baseball idols, first hand."
—Tom Stevens, Babe Ruth's grandson

Babe Ruth and Lou Gehrig pose with members of the Fresno Athletic Club Japanese American team before a barnstorming exhibition game in Fresno, California, October 29, 1927. "Barnstorming" is a term that originated with theater troupes that traveled around the country, often performing in barns. In the same way, after the regular season, pro baseball players traveled the country playing local teams, college teams, and each other, giving baseball fans an opportunity to see their favorite players in action.

The Nisei Baseball League was the second-generation Japanese American baseball league. Like the Negro Leaguers, the Nisei Leaguers, also top-notch players, were not allowed to play in the major leagues. While those were the MLB rules, Babe made it clear on barnstorming tours and otherwise that he didn't abide by them.

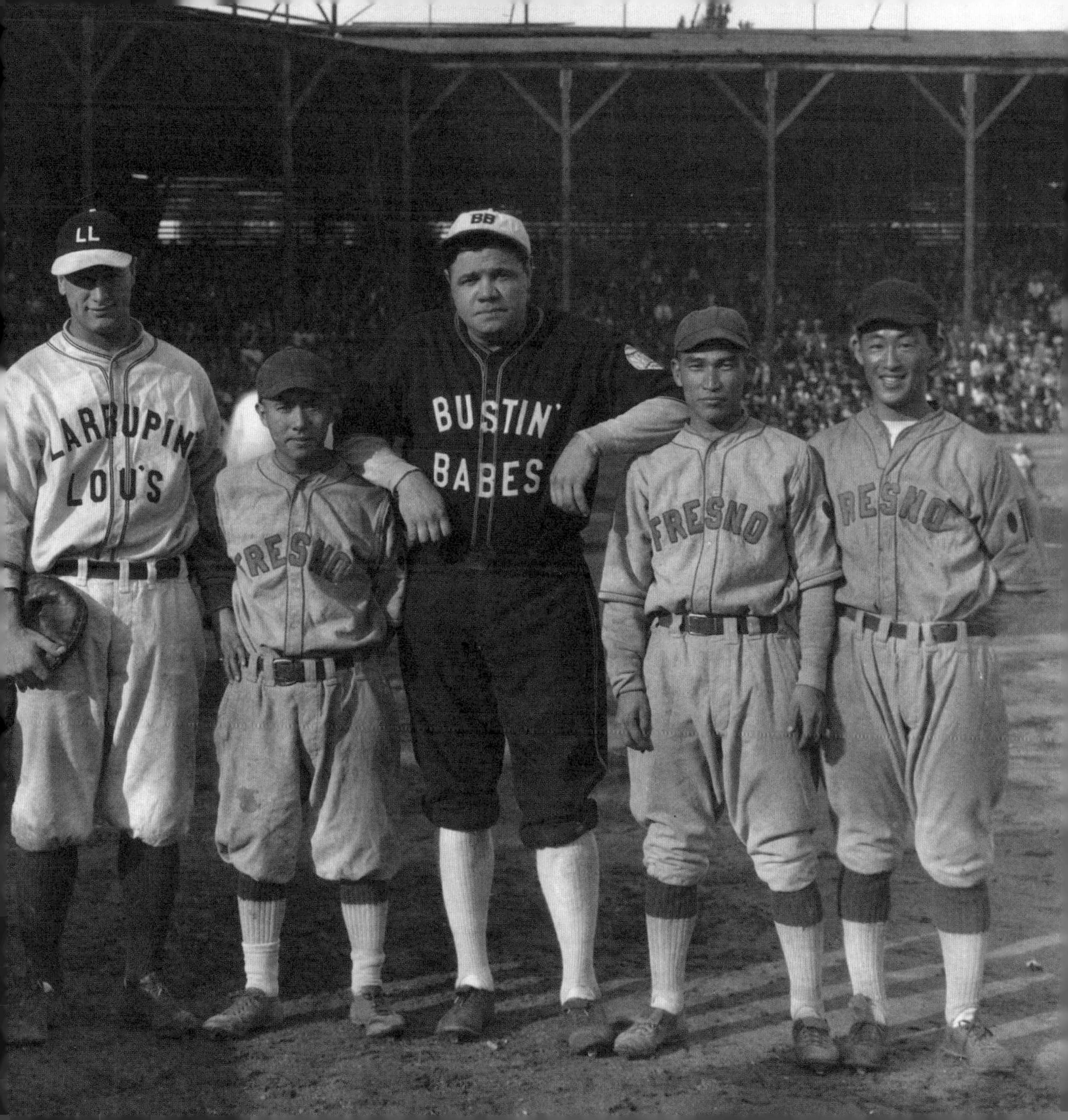
LL
LARRUPIN'
LOU'S
FRESNO
BB
BUSTIN'
BABES
FRESNO
FRESNO

"DID I WANT TO PLAY BASEBALL? DOES A FISH LIKE TO SWIM OR A SQUIRREL CLIMB TREES?"

"Sometimes I pitched. Sometimes I caught, and frequently I played the outfield and infield. It was all the same to me. All I wanted was to play. I didn't care much where."
—George Herman Ruth in *Babe Ruth's Own Book of Baseball*

Young George on the ballfield at St. Mary's, circa 1911.

WHY BABE?

BEFORE SUPERMAN, BATMAN, THE GREEN LANTERN, OR EVEN BUCK ROGERS, THERE WAS GEORGE HERMAN "BABE" RUTH: PART SUPERHERO, PART FOLK LEGEND, FULL-ON ACTION FIGURE.

"To understand him you had to understand this: he wasn't human."
—"Jumping Joe" Dugan

During his first six seasons in professional baseball, Babe Ruth was one of the sport's most successful pitchers—winning eighty-nine games and three World Series games—while at the same time making a name for himself as a powerhouse slugger. In 1919, his sixth season—still pitching regularly—the Babe hit twenty-nine homers to set a new all-time single-season home run record—a record he set and broke and set and broke and set until he finally maxed out at sixty home runs in the 1927 season—four homers more than any other entire team's season total that year, except the Yankees, of course.

"He hits the ball harder and further than any man I ever saw."
—Hall of Famer Bill Dickey

Even now, more than one hundred years since Babe Ruth set his first pitching record and at least eighty years since he belted his last homer, players are still being measured by standards he set and still chasing his records. And even today, with all the improvements in uniforms and equipment, fitness, and training techniques, most ballplayers fall short. Not only was Babe the first MLB player to rack up cumulative milestones of two hundred, then three hundred, then four hundred and so on to over seven hundred home runs, according to the current *Baseball Almanac*, his records for "most home runs in any decade (467 in the 1920s), fastest player to hit 600 home runs (2,044 games) and fastest player to hit 700 home runs (2,418 games)" have yet to be broken. And those aren't the only ones!

> "Some 20 years ago, I stopped talking about the Babe for the simple reason that I realized that those who had never seen him didn't believe me."
> —Sportswriter Tommy Holmes to Red Smith on the day of Babe Ruth's funeral.

But why? And how? At six feet, two inches, Babe stood tall. In 1920, the average height for a man was five feet, eight inches. And he was big. Weighing in at about 185 pounds when he started playing pro ball, "George" outweighed the average American male by about thirty pounds. But he wasn't the only big, tall, strong player. Nor was he the smartest, most handsome, or toughest of them all. He was good at sports and, maybe most importantly, he was a good sport. Having lived, from age seven to nineteen in a home for orphaned, neglected, and delinquent boys, he was well-schooled in sportsmanship. And he loved baseball! From the first time he watched Brother Matthias, an Xaverian Brother at St. Mary's Industrial School, toss a baseball into the air, take a swing, and send the fungo whizzing—like a bird or a plane or rocket—George Herman Ruth knew that's what he wanted to do.

> "I think I was born as a hitter the first day I ever saw him [Brother Matthias] hit a baseball."
> —Babe Ruth to Bob Considine in *The Babe Ruth Story*, 1948.

Baseball was America's sport in those days. As Hall of Famer Hank Greenberg noted in *The Story of My Life*, "Football was in its infancy, basketball was nonexistent, tennis was for the newly rich and ne'er-do-wells, and hockey was a Canadian sport that hadn't invaded the United States. Baseball was the game, and all the athletes who had any talent at all tried to make a career in professional baseball. That was the kind of competition the Babe was up against."

"Go big or go home!" No one knows who coined the term to encourage bold risk-taking. Regardless of who said it first, the Great Bambino lived it.

"Long before Palmer or Jordan, Woods or Ali, Babe Ruth smothered America with his presence.
And he did it at a time where there was no television, computers, cell phones, Internet, coffee bars or ESPN."
—Mike Barnicle, ESPN the Magazine, September 14, 1999

Babe was bigger than life, but at the same time, he was a regular guy who happened to get lucky and knew it. He was a superstar almost from the moment he, Jack Dunn's "newest baby," arrived at his first spring training in Fayetteville, North Carolina, and astounded everyone by hitting a homer so far—from Cape Fear Fairgrounds into a cornfield or pond (the story varies)—it broke a town distance record set by mega-athlete, Olympian Jim Thorpe, in 1909. Unlike some other players, however, the Babe embraced his celebrity—always out to have a good time and put on a good show. Once he turned pro, rarely a day passed that the Babe wasn't in the news. And even though he's been gone more than seventy-five years, it's much the same today—during baseball season and otherwise.

"He was the original larger-than-life sports hero and he became the
first of many athletes to be known on a first-name basis."
—Christine Brennan, "First Dominant Hero Still No. 1: The Babe,"
USA Today, December 31, 1999

Something George Herman "Babe" Ruth was not, was reserved. Good, bad, or sideways—Babe told it, and told it like it was. There are reels and rolls, pages and volumes, of interviews, articles, and books about Babe, the Bambino, The Sultan of Swat, the Mastodon of Mash, King of Crash, etc. etc. And books by him and ghostwritten for him, including pamphlets tucked into bubblegum packets and cereal boxes. One could spend months and years sifting through it all. Many of Babe's oft-repeated quotes are about baseball, certainly. At the same time, much of what Babe said about failure and success, perseverance, and what really matters, applies to everything: giving one's best and living one's best life.

"Ruth isn't a man; he's an institution."
—Moe Berg

The Babe sparring with his personal trainer, Artie McGovern, in 1942.

Members of the Boston Red Sox, circa 1916.
Left to right: George H. "Babe" Ruth, Ernie Shore, George "Rube" Foster, and Dellos "Del" Gainer.

"A FELLOW HAS TO HAVE SOMETHING BESIDES CURLY HAIR ABOUT HIS SHOULDERS. HE'S GOT TO KNOW HIS ONIONS."

"I get back to the dugout and they ask me what it was I hit and I tell them I don't know except it looked good."
—Babe Ruth's Own Book of Baseball

"They [home runs] come at a rate of one in every 30 major league at-bats now; in Ruth's heyday they came at a rate of every 91 at-bats."
—Eric Brady, USA Today, August 6, 1999

"YOU'VE GOT TO CHASE THEM, AND CHASE THEM, AND CHASE THEM SOME MORE. PRACTICE AND PRACTICE ALONE WILL DO IT."

"The real outfielder studies the hitters as closely as does the pitcher. They shift with every man who comes to the plate, moving in and back and to and fro like a lot of policeman looking for a riot."
— *Babe Ruth's Own Book of Baseball*

Babe Ruth going back for a catch in Yankee Stadium, early 1920s.

"THE GREATEST CURVE BALL IN THE WORLD ISN'T WORTH A THIN DIME IF YOU DON'T KNOW WHAT TO DO WITH IT."

"When you're great, you're great. It's when you come up with Ruth, you come up with Josh Gibson, you come up with Satchel. You just say 'great'."
—Buck O'Neill, player-manager. MLB's First African American Coach

Josh and The Babe by sports artist Bill Purdom, commissioned by Sean Gibson and Brent Stevens, the great-grandsons of Josh Gibson and Babe Ruth, respectively. Josh Gibson—primarily a catcher, a great all-around player, and likely the most powerful hitter in the Negro Leagues—was often referred to as the "Black Babe Ruth." After a chance meeting, Sean and Brent began to wonder: What if Josh and the Babe had the opportunity to play against each other? No doubt these two baseball superstars of their respective professional leagues would have welcomed the opportunity. Even now they hold the record for the highest career slugging percentages (SLG) in major league history—Josh Gibson with .718; Babe Ruth with .690 (and well over .700 in seasons he wasn't pitching). Alas, the two Hall of Famers never had the chance to play against each other, and as far as we know, never met. But what a game that might have been!

"DON'T EVER FORGET TWO THINGS I'M GOING TO TELL YOU. ONE, DON'T BELIEVE EVERYTHING THAT'S WRITTEN ABOUT YOU. TWO, DON'T PICK UP TOO MANY CHECKS."

The Babe's first motion picture, *Headin' Home* (1920), in which he played a character similar to himself, was filmed mostly at night at Biograph Studios in Fort Lee, New Jersey. On August 22, 1920, action scenes were filmed at a ballfield made up to look like the Polo Grounds. A crowd of two thousand movie extras were in the stands as "fans." While the cameras rolled, Babe Ruth's character (also called "Babe") used a bat he supposedly whittled out of a tree trunk to blast balls out of the park and into neighboring houses and yards. After filming that day, he raced back to the real Polo Grounds for a Yankees' game against the Detroit Tigers. During the real game, in three at-bats, Babe didn't get any hits, but he did manage two bases on balls (BB); the Yankees lost 9–11.

A production still from the silent movie *Babe Comes Home* starring Babe Ruth and Anna Q. Nilsson, directed by Ted Wilde (1927). Note the mouse trap stuck on his finger. Babe appeared in five feature-length movies and six "shorts," as well as instructional films and countless newsreels.

"I SWING BIG, WITH EVERYTHING I'VE GOT. I HIT BIG OR I MISS BIG."

"Peerless 'Babe' Hangs Up New World's Record." In the doubleheader against the Washington Senators on June 2, 1920, Babe hit three home runs—two in the first game, one in the second. He was the first player to hit three home runs in a game in both the American League (with the NY Yankees in 1930) and the National League (with the Boston Braves in 1935).

Inset: Babe posing shirtless in the locker room.

"GOOD PITCHING IS PITCHING THAT PREVENTS RUNS, REGARDLESS OF BASE HITS."

"As soon as I got out there I felt a strange relationship with the pitcher's mound. It was as if I'd been born out there. Pitching just felt like the most natural thing in the world. Striking out batters was easy."
—*Babe Ruth's Own Book of Baseball*

"This Ruthless Ruth, the stem-winder, is some hurler. A pitcher who is so versatile that he can not only shoot all sorts of deliveries from the port turret, but can besides all this hit a home run, and a couple of incidental singles in one game is some asset, ladies and gentlemen, some asset indeed."
—Wilmot Giffin, *NY Evening Journal*, May 6, 1915

Babe top-row center in 1914 Providence Grays team photo.

"ALL THE BASE HITS IN THE WORLD ARE WASTED IF THE HITTER DOESN'T COMPLETE HIS JOURNEY AND CHECK IN AT THE HOME PLATE WITH A RUN."

"Give any ball club a second baseman and shortstop who can work together in perfect harmony with each knowing the other's style and methods and you've solved four-fifths of the infield troubles right there."
—*Babe Ruth's Own Book of Baseball*

"CONFIDENCE IS ONE OF THE BIGGEST THINGS IN HITTING."

"When Ruth's time at bat is over and it's my turn the fans are still buzzing about what Babe did, regardless of whether he belted a home run or struck out. They wouldn't notice it if I walked up to home plate on my hands, stood on my head, and held the bat between my toes."
—Lou Gehrig, *The Babe: The Game that Ruth Built*

Jimmie Foxx, Babe Ruth, Lou Gehrig, and Al Simmons before a 1929 Athletics–Yankee game in Philadelphia. That was the first year Yankees' players wore numbers on their uniforms. Numbers were assigned according to batting order: #1 Earle Combs, #2 Mark Koenig, #3 Babe Ruth, #4 Lou Gehrig, #5 Bob Meusel, and so on. Aside from rare occasions when they switched things up, Gehrig followed Ruth to the plate.

"I'VE NEVER HEARD A CROWD BOO A HOMER, BUT I'VE HEARD PLENTY OF BOOS AFTER A STRIKEOUT."

After his disappointing 1922 season, Babe spent the winter with his family at Home Plate Farm in Sudbury, Massachusetts, where—true to his promise—he "shaped up" by chopping and hauling wood. While with the Red Sox, he often arranged for busloads of orphans to visit the farm for a day-long picnic and ball game, making sure each kid left with a glove and autographed baseball.

Babe Ruth carrying a 300 pound log for the stove, in snow. Home Plate Farm, winter 1922.

JUST GEORGE

"World's worse singer, world's best pitcher."
—Inscription inside George Herman Ruth's 1910-era hymnal from St. Mary's

I was a bad kid" is how Babe Ruth described himself. His sister, Mamie, the only other of seven siblings to survive past infancy, disagreed. "Little George wasn't really bad, he was just full of mischief" is how she described her big brother. "He was hard to control and couldn't resist a dare. If you dared him to do something, consider it done."

There were a lot of dares made and taken in the rough harbor area of southwest Baltimore where George Herman Ruth Jr. started out. He was born on February 6, 1895, in the upstairs front bedroom of his grandparents' house at 216 Emory Street (now the Babe Ruth Birthplace Museum). It was just a few blocks west of today's Oriole Park at Camden Yards in Pigtown (so-called because pigs were run through its streets from the stockyard to the slaughterhouses). Babe's father, George Senior, a former lightning rod salesman, ran a saloon. His mother, Katherine, "Katie," a tiny, frail woman, helped in the saloon and kept house.

"He was a waif on the Baltimore waterfront at the turn of the century. The chances of him becoming world famous were about the odds of winning the lottery."
—Michael Gibbons, Executive Director of the Babe Ruth Birthplace Museum

At the time, Baltimore was the sixth largest city in the country and a major port. Pigtown, a noisy bustling community with cargo ships, fisherman, dock workers, and horse-drawn wagons coming and going, provided plenty of action to keep a curious boy busy. And for a boy who was looking—with busy parents who weren't—Pigtown offered plenty of ways to get into trouble. And George did!

"I had a rotten start . . . I spent most of the first seven years living over my father's saloon. When I wasn't living over it, I was living in it, studying the rough talk of the longshoremen, merchant sailors, roustabouts, and water-front bums. When I wasn't living in it I was living in the neighborhood streets."
—Babe Ruth in *The Babe Ruth Story*

When he was seven, George was declared "incorrigible" and sent to St. Mary's Industrial School for Orphans, Delinquent, Incorrigible, and Wayward Boys. It was a five-story brick building surrounded by a tall wall with an iron-gated entrance that looked and felt much like a prison. In fact, the eight hundred boys living there, between the ages of five and twenty-one, called themselves "inmates."

> "There's no use of my beating around the bush. I spent twelve years in a reform school."
> —*Playing the Game: My Early Years in Baseball* by Babe Ruth

St. Mary's was run by the Xaverian Brothers, an order of the Catholic Church, which set strict rules: The boys were up each morning at 6 a.m., had breakfast, attended Mass, and were in class by 7:30 a.m., where, along with the usual school subjects, they were taught a trade. As it turned out, George—"Jidge" as his friends called him—had a knack for shirt making. Years later, long after becoming "Babe," his wife, Claire, noted how he would still mend his own shirts and sew on buttons.

Back in those days, before child labor laws restricted it, most poorer children worked alongside adults. George and the other boys at St. Mary's were no exception. After school, he worked at the Oppenheim, Oberndorf & Co. Shirt Factory, about three miles away. "I was a joiner and he put collars on," fellow "inmate" Lawton Stenersen recalled. "We got six cents a shirt." On paydays, most of their wages were turned over to the Brothers, who saved them so the boys would have a nest egg to start out on when they left St. Mary's.

At first, George found living at St. Mary's tough. The rules chafed. And because he hadn't learned to read or write yet, and had trouble staying focused, he was put in class with the younger students, which felt especially embarrassing.

> "In his first years at St. Mary's, he ran away three times—escapes he later called his 'parole'."
> —Babe's daughter, Julia Ruth Stevens, *Babe Ruth: Remembering the Bambino*

Sports and a bat-wielding six-foot, six-inch giant, Brother Matthias Boutlier, proved to be George's salvation. Each afternoon and on Sundays the boys had recreation time during which they ice-skated and played basketball, volleyball and especially baseball. Brother Matthias was head of discipline at St. Mary's. He was a firm disciplinarian, but he was also fair and kind. And boy, could he wallop a baseball! Brother Matthias would take hold of the bat with one giant hand, toss a baseball into the air, and, on the way down, give it a mighty smack that set that fungo flying with all the boys scrambling to catch it. George had never seen anything like it. Brother Matthias, likewise, noticed what a fine natural athlete George was and started coaching him, correcting his stance and teaching him to catch and pitch.

"It was at St. Mary's that I met and learned to love the greatest man I've ever known. His name was Brother Matthias. He was the father I needed. He taught me to read and write—and he taught me the difference in right and wrong." —Babe Ruth, *The Baseball Anthology*

A gifted athlete, George caught on quickly. At St. Mary's, there were more than forty teams organized by age and ability levels, Red Sox, White Sox, Cubs, Giants, etc.— that played against teams from throughout the surrounding area. By the time he was eight or nine, George played with eleven- and twelve-year-olds; by the time he was twelve, he was playing with sixteen-year-olds; and by the time he was sixteen, George was playing on the St. Mary's Red Sox traveling team.

During his final year at St. Mary's, George was given permission to leave school on weekends and play with other teams. He was hitting home runs in practically every game and being written up in the local paper. That's when, with help from Brother Gilbert at St. Mary's, Jack Dunn, owner and manager of the Baltimore Orioles (at the time, a minor-league team in the International League), caught wind of him: A southpaw pitching, switch-hitter with a batting average of .537, who could also catch *and* field He had to see this "Ruth" kid for himself!

One afternoon George was called into St. Mary's office. Jesse Linthicum, sportswriter for **The Baltimore Sun**, was there that fortuitous day. In a 1948 article titled "Babe Ruth, 'A Natural,'" he recalled how George showed up accompanied by a handful of teammates and some young tag-alongs. Although Dunn had never seen George play, he had a reputation for being able to judge a player just by the way they carried themselves. On the spot, he offered George a contract. And just that fast, George accepted. In unison, the St. Mary's players groaned, "There goes our ball club."

On February 27, 1914, George Herman Ruth Jr. signed a contract to play for Jack Dunn's Baltimore Orioles at a salary of $25 per week. Compared to what rookie ballplayers earn today, $25 a week, $100 per month, $600 for the season, sounds like peanuts. But, in a time when a movie ticket cost seven cents, a good pair of shoes about $3.50, and a brand-new Dodge Brothers Touring Car went for $500, it was a fortune.

> "I went out and celebrated, just as soon as I got my first paycheck—$100. I bought a bicycle, something that I had wanted and often prayed for through most of my young life."
> —Babe Ruth in *The Babe Ruth Story*

Less than three weeks earlier, George had celebrated what he thought was his twentieth birthday but was actually his nineteenth. For most of his life, Babe believed his birthday was February 7, 1894. It wasn't until 1934, when he obtained a copy of his birth certificate so he could apply for a passport, that he found out he had actually been born on February 6, 1895. What he thought was his twentieth birthday marked his last year at St. Mary's. To suddenly go from believing he faced a future spent sewing shirts for six cents a collar to being offered big money to play baseball, Babe must have felt like he'd struck gold.

"I'D GIVE A YEAR OF MY LIFE IF I COULD HIT A HOMERUN ON OPENING DAY OF THIS GREAT NEW PARK."

April 18, 1923, Yankee Stadium hosted its first season opener: NY Yankees vs. Boston Red Sox. True to his wish, Babe did hit a homer that day. The first baseball game ever played in Yankee Stadium ended with a score of 4–1, Yankees. Babe Ruth went on to hit forty-four home runs that season, leading the Yankees to win a third straight American League Pennant and the team's first World Series Championship. Because so many fans attended Yankees games mostly to watch Babe Ruth play, Yankee Stadium was nicknamed "The House That Ruth Built."

"GEE, IT'S LONESOME IN THE OUTFIELD. IT'S HARD TO KEEP AWAKE WITH NOTHING TO DO."

"When you consider ballplayers are together from February until October, there are going to be squabbles. But Babe and Lou enemies? Not a chance. Babe was an extrovert in the extreme and Lou was an introvert. Babe threw his money around and Lou counted his pennies. Babe liked the high life and Lou enjoyed the opera and the philharmonic. Babe was glib with the press; Lou found it hard to come up with a snappy quip. There may have been comments here and there that caused temporary chagrin, but Babe and Lou were teammates and friends on and off the field. The press created a feud between Ruth and Gehrig that I never saw. Babe and Lou were both dear friends of mine as well as teammates, and I respected the fact that they lived life their own way. Nothing more, nothing less."
—Lefty Gomez, *An American Odyssey* by Vernona Gomez
and Lawrence Goldstone.

October 12, 1928, Dexter Park, Woodhaven, Queens, the Babe and Lou Gehrig whooped it up at a "rodeo" benefit for Broad Street Hospital.

"PLAY HARD, PLAY FAST, BUT PLAY FAIR."

"Black or White, our common hero was George Herman (Babe) Ruth. Every kid was ready to knock down the friend or foe who denied his personal claim to being Babe Ruth."
—Lucius Jones, *Atlanta Daily World*, April 12, 1942

"Boys Jam Trenton Field and Stop Game When Ruth Hits His Third Homer of Day," **The New York Times**, October 12, 1927.

Babe Ruth's All-Stars, including Lou Gehrig, began their 1927 barnstorming tour with a two-game series against the Brooklyn Royal Giants, a formidable Negro Leagues team led by manager-pitcher Dick "Cannon Ball" Redding. News accounts of the October 11 game at Trenton Field agreed that Cannon Ball's blazing fastball was virtually unhittable through the first five innings. After Babe flied out and popped out his first two at-bats, the **Trenton State Gazette** reported him as saying, "I'll hit one off this baby yet. I pretty near got a hold of that last one. I'm hitting under 'em. But I'll meet the next one on the nose." True to his word, in the sixth inning, Babe launched one over four hundred feet to deep right centerfield, and in the very next frame drove one one-hundred feet farther, clearing a three-story house in right center. (In fairness to the thirty-four-year-old Redding, he was surely running out of gas by that time.) This photograph, believed to have been taken at that game, shows Babe with a Brooklyn Royal Giant's catcher, likely John Cason.

As described by an October 12 **New York Times** article, both games were raucous and rowdy: "Twice before the eighth inning, as Ruth lifted the ball over the right field wall, hundreds of boys swarmed into the field to romp from third to home with the King of Swat, each time holding up the game for fifteen minutes before the field could be cleared. However, after his third homer in the eighth with two on base, officials found it impossible to get the fans from the field and the game was called."

"WATCH MY DUST."

"The Babe had played with Black teams against Black teams, with White teams against Black teams, with White against White. He was a nondenominational, nondiscriminatory belter . . . If you were a pretty good baseball player in the Twenties, professional or amateur, big-city or small-town, the chances were pretty good that you played against Babe Ruth at least once in your life. If you didn't, it was your fault. You probably missed the invitation."
—Leigh Montville, *The Big Bam: The Life and Times of Babe Ruth*

A promotional card produced for "Carl Mays Stars" ill-fated 1921 barnstorming tour. As the name suggests, the team, which was supposed to include several Yankees, was contracted to play a host of postseason games. However, several players, including Mays, dropped out after receiving warning letters signed by Baseball Commissioner Judge Kenesaw Mountain Landis forbidding players from pennant-winning teams "to participate as individuals or as a team in exhibition games during the year in which the world's championship was decided."

Along with Bob Muesel, Bill Piercy, and former teammate Tom Sheehan, Babe ignored the warning and set off on the barnstorming tour. As punishment, Commissioner Landis suspended Ruth and Muesel for the first forty days of the 1922 season and fined them their full World Series bonus, about $3500 each. Because Sheehan and Piercy hadn't been on the Yankees' World Series roster, they weren't punished. In July of 1922, the barnstorming rule was amended to allow pennant winners to participate in postseason exhibition games—with permission.

SPECIAL TOUR
BABE RUTH, CARL MAYS STARS
Direction Jess Lynch, Savage Enterprises
370 East 149th St. N.Y. City.

"THE FANS WOULD RATHER SEE ME HIT ONE HOMER TO RIGHT THAN THREE DOUBLES TO LEFT."

"Times have changed. Some years ago it would have been a serious offense for any of us to break a window with a baseball. Now it brings a new automobile."
—Babe Ruth

Babe Ruth posing outside Wells Motor Company on October 6, 1926, after hitting three home runs in Game Four of the 1926 World Series against the St. Louis Cardinals. Babe's three homers that game was a World Series first.

The second homer Ruth hit that game flew over the right field pavilion, out of Sportsman's Park, and onto the street. The ball took one bounce and broke the showroom window of the Wells Motor Company, bounded off a Chevrolet Coupe and back onto the street, and then kept rolling until a boy snatched it up. Later the boy, along with two others, showed up at the Yankee clubhouse—each clutching one of the home run baseballs. Babe signed and labeled the baseballs: "No. 1," "No. 2," and "No. 3."

Wells Motors gave Babe the undamaged Chevy Coupe the ball had hit and had commemorative steering wheels made. Customers who bought a car from the Wells Motor Company were given the option: with or without the "Babe Ruth Steering Wheel."

"PITCHING, AFTER ALL, IS ABOUT ONE-THIRD ARM WORK AND TWO-THIRDS HEAD WORK."

"His [Babe's] chief stock in trade is speed, but he also has a sharp-breaking curve and a tantalizing slow ball."
—*The Boston Globe*, July 10, 1914 (the day before Babe Ruth's Red Sox pitching debut)

Babe Ruth pitching at Majestic Park, during spring training in Hot Springs, Arkansas, 1915. Babe Ruth was one of the best southpaw pitchers in Red Sox history. How good a pitcher was he? Babe held the record as being the only player with more than five hundred strikeouts as a pitcher and more than one hundred home runs as a hitter until LA Angels Shohei Ohtani broke his 501-record in 2023—a record that had held for eighty-eight seasons!

Renowned for its mineral baths, Hot Springs was the "birthplace" of spring training. Beginning in 1886 with the Chicago White Stockings (now the Cubs) and through the 1940s, teams from all the leagues—with rosters that included many future Hall of Famers—trained and played throughout the city. It was the epicenter of Black baseball. Hot Springs Historic Baseball Trail marks the locations.

January 30, 1930, Palm Beach, Florida. Babe and his wife, Claire, mugging with fans at Sea Spray Beach before he reported to spring training.

"I HAVE ONLY ONE SUPERSTITION. I TOUCH ALL THE BASES WHEN I HIT A HOME RUN."

"There was buried in Ruth humanitarianism beyond belief, an intelligence he was never given credit for, a childish desire to be over-virile, living up to credits given his home-run power—and yet a need for intimate affection and respect, and a feverish desire to play baseball, perform, act and live a life he didn't and couldn't take time to understand."
—Waite Hoyt

"A GOOD PLAYER NEVER STOPS UNTIL HE'S ACTUALLY OUT."

On July 5, 1924, in the fourth inning of the first game in a doubleheader against the Washington Senators, Babe ran full force into the wall at Griffith Stadium while chasing down a fly ball and knocked himself out. After remaining unconscious for about five minutes, they splashed water on his face to revive him. Babe not only stayed in the game, but he ended up three-for-three with two doubles. He also played in the nightcap.

As for the ball he was chasing? It fell foul.

"WEALTH IS ALWAYS ATTRACTED, NEVER PURSUED."

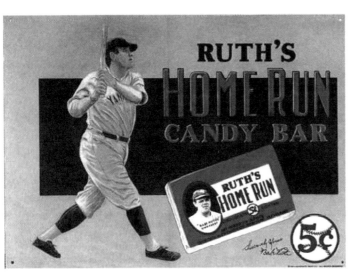

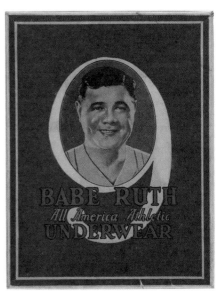

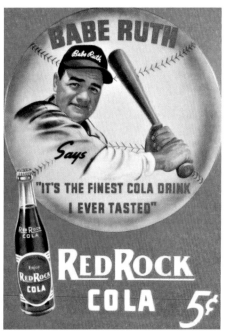

Bats, breakfast cereal, undies, gum, cola, gasoline . . . you name it, Babe Ruth endorsed it. And yes, Babe did have a candy bar named after him. It was "Ruth's Home Run Candy Bar" created by the George H. Ruth Candy Co. in 1926. Capitalizing on the Babe's fame, in 1921 the Curtiss Candy Company changed its "Kandy Kake" bar and renamed it "Baby Ruth." But when challenged in court, the company claimed their candy was named after a baby born in the White House thirty years earlier: Grover Cleveland's daughter Ruth.

When it comes to baseball cards, the Babe is tops there too. During his career, more than two hundred different versions of baseball cards featuring Babe Ruth were issued—still more after he retired. In 2021, a mint condition 1933 Babe Ruth Big League card, like the one pictured above, sold for more than 5 million dollars.

BABE IN TOYLAND

"This Baby will never get away from me."
—Jack Dunn

On February 27, 1914, George Herman Ruth Jr. bounded out the gates of St. Mary's (wanting to avoid a pinch that might wake him from this incredible dream). He was on his way to the train station. Destination: Fayetteville, North Carolina, and the Baltimore Orioles Training Camp.

Barely nineteen, George had never been on a train before. Prior to that day, the only motorized vehicle he'd been on was a trolley between St. Mary's Industrial School and Pigtown those few times he had returned home. Imagine the world back then: no paved highways with cars zooming back and forth or trucks or planes flying overhead. There were few cars on the road—in 1910, there were about five cars for every one thousand people in America. To get around, folks living in Baltimore and other big cities took the trolley, walked, pedaled bicycles, or rode in horse-drawn wagons or carriages. And for longer distances, trains and boats were the only way to travel. Though telephones were in use, at most there was one phone per household firmly tethered to the wall. There were no radios—speech would be transmitted for the first time in 1915, from San Francisco to New York City. Television hadn't been invented yet. Neither had batting helmets, windshield wipers, tennis shoes, zippers, or Double-Bubble Chewing Gum. There were movies, but only silent ones. And for young George, who'd spent most of his life thus far with every decision made for him, there was freedom!

Biographer Leigh Montville wrote how George, "Jidge" in the local vernacular, acted and ate "like a man released from prison." After a childhood of miserly meals that never left him feeling full, Babe felt like he had a lot of catching up to do when it came to eating. In his 1948 autobiography, Babe recounted the moment when the realization of exactly how much his life had changed hit him— right where it counted. It was one of his first mornings at Orioles camp. He was with the team in a hotel studying the breakfast menu. Considering it was one of the first times he'd ever held a menu, let alone been given a choice of what to eat, he was having a tough time deciding. Noticing this, one of the other players told him to order anything he wanted because the club paid for meals during spring training. Babe couldn't believe it.

> "I was on my third stack of wheat cakes and third order of ham, and I hadn't even come up for air, when I realized that some of the other fellows were watching me. I looked at them silently, and kept chewing."
> —Babe Ruth in *The Babe Ruth Story*

While he may have looked and acted like a uncouth pup, rookie Ruth's performance on the field surpassed Jack Dunn's and everyone else's expectations. Jesse Linthicum reported how Ruth—who happened to be playing shortstop because that early in spring training only pitchers and catchers had arrived, so they filled in at various positions to practice—"handled all fielding chances with ease and grace." And how, on the team's first inter-squad game, "the youngster" made an "immediate impression" on everyone watching when he blasted the Thorpe-record-breaking 405-foot "cornfield" homer—"a prodigious clout that sent the locals down to main street talking to themselves."

On the walk back to the hotel after the game, Linthicum overheard Jack Dunn say, "This Baby will never get away from me." Linthicum later wrote, "Then and there, Ruth acquired the nickname of 'Babe.'" A highway marker on Gillespie Street in Fayetteville, North Carolina, memorializes both occasions:

As astonishing as Babe's batting was, many fans found his let-it-rip style off-putting—wrong even! Swinging hard to hit big meant striking out and that's not what baseball was about back then. Home runs were so rare in fact, that Frank "Home Run" Baker, the leading hitter of the time, never hit more than twelve home runs in a season. This was Baseball's Deadball Era—or as it's called "small ball"—the years between the turn of the century and 1920, when the game was mostly about what went on in the infield. Pitchers scuffed, chipped, spit on, and smacked baseballs to make them less round so their trajectory would be less predictable. Batters choked up on the bat to gain more control and, rather than swinging hard with an eye to the sky, they bunted, chopped, and purposefully placed the ball with the goal of getting on base and helping teammates advance bases—more hit-and-run and stealing, less power hitting. Clearly Brother Matthias never gave Babe that memo, and Jack Dunn had no intention of sharing it with him.

"The more I see Ruth the hitter, the more I like him."
—Jack Dunn to Jesse Linthicum, *Baltimore Sun*

As soon as he was given a chance, Babe wowed them with his pitching too. During his first time on the mound, Babe "fanned four batters in three innings." But, reporters noted, while he had terrific speed, he lacked experience going up against big-league hitters. He was a fast learner though—in his first pitching start, Babe scored a win against the Phillies in an exhibition game. He soon became the Orioles' star pitcher. Sportswriters reported Ruth "tossed like a million dollars" and had the visiting teams "breaking their backs in an effort to reach his benders."

Back in Baltimore, high on accolades from his spring training performance, Jack Dunn's "Baby" rejoiced in his new-found freedom. With practice and game times his only concern, he explored the city, taking full advantage of all that city life offered. From his hotel room, he'd watch the trains go by, or rode elevators, sometimes begging the operator to let him work the controls. And as often as not, when Babe finished practice with the Orioles, he'd hightail it back to St. Mary's to play a few innings with teammates there.

Jack Dunn, the Orioles owner/manager—as well as George's legal guardian—tried to impose rules, but George wasn't having them. After spending all those years almost exclusively in the company of boys—more than eight hundred boys governed by the strict Catholic Brothers—young George must have felt like a "babe" set loose in Toyland. He had wheels, jingle in his pocket, girls to see, and places to be!

While the Babe was having the time of his life on and off the field, Jack Dunn's Orioles were in trouble. Despite being first in the International League and in line to win the pennant, the fans weren't showing up to the Orioles games. There was a new team in town, the Terrapins of the Federal League, with a brand-new ballpark, and fans were flocking to their games instead. Dunn petitioned the International League to let him move the Orioles to Richmond, Virginia, but was turned down. He was faced with a tough choice: break up the team or lose it. Midway through the season, he sold three players to the Boston Red Sox for $25,000: pitcher Ernie Shore, catcher Ben Egan, and—despite his "newest baby" having won fourteen of twenty games for his first-place Orioles—Babe Ruth.

"When the ball was last seen crossing the roof of the stand in deep right field at 315 feet, we wondered whether new baseballs in the original package ever remark: 'Join Ruth and see the world.'
—Grantland Rice

"THE ABILITY TO TAG FAST AND GET AWAY HAS SAVED MANY A PAIR OF SHINS."

"Babe Ruth still can hit the dirt," *The New York World-Telegram*, August 14, 1934; the Babe sliding into home plate during the first game of a doubleheader against the Detroit Tigers at Yankee Stadium. Shown in the photo are Cleveland shortstop Ray Chapman, catcher Ray Hayworth, and umpire Lou Kolls. Dramatic as it was, Ruth's run didn't make a difference; the Yanks lost both games.

CHAPMAN

RUTH

HAYWORTH

UMPIRE
KOLLS

"LIFE IS A GAME LIKE ANY OTHER; WE JUST DON'T TAKE IT AS SERIOUSLY."

Freewheeling Babe, circa 1914. For Babe, who'd spent most of his life as one of St. Mary's "inmates," freedom and speed were a heady combination. As one story goes, shortly after buying a bicycle with his first paycheck, he was careening around a corner and almost ran over his boss, Orioles' owner Jack Dunn. Babe swerved and crashed into the back of a hay wagon. After checking that his star player wasn't injured, Dunn gave him a piece of his mind: "If you want to go back home, kid, just keep riding those bikes."

"YOU CAN HAVE THE NINE GREATEST INDIVIDUAL BALL PLAYERS IN THE WORLD, BUT IF THEY DON'T PLAY TOGETHER THE CLUB WON'T BE WORTH A DIME."

Reporters dubbed the first six batters in the Yankees' lineup—Earle Combs, Mark Koenig, Babe Ruth, Lou Gehrig, Bob Meusel, and Tony Lazzeri—"Murderers' Row" because they were all formidable hitters and because of the way they routinely started banging out hits in the second half of the game, right around 5 p.m., which became known as "Five O'Clock Lightning."

Why 5 p.m.? In the days before lighted ballparks, games started about 3:30, so by the fifth or sixth innings, around 5 p.m., hitters had had plenty of time to study the pitcher and the pitcher would have begun to tire out.

1927 New York Yankees team-autographed print.

"YOU KNOW A GAME OF BASEBALL IS LIKE A BATTLE . . . JUST LIKE WAR, IT'S A BATTLE OF DEFENSE AGAINST OFFENSE AND THE BEST ORGANIZA- TION WINS."

"The mere presence of Babe created a disastrous psychological problem for the other team."
—Yankee Manager Miller Huggins in *I'd Rather Be a Yankee* by John Tullius

In May of 1924, Babe enlisted in the Army National Guard, 104th Field Artillery Unit. His primary job was to raise awareness of the Citizens' Training Program. Nine days later, he was sent to Washington D.C. to meet General John J. Pershing. This photo of "Private Ruth" snapping a salute is one of a series of publicity photos taken on May 29, 1924.

"WHEN I'M IN A SLUMP, ONE OF THE FIRST THINGS I DO IS START TAKING THE FIRST ONE."

During their 1927 Home Run Race, Babe—the "King of Swing"—and Lou Gehrig—the "Prince of Pow"—hammed it up plenty for the press. In one radio comedy sketch, Gehrig, often on the receiving end of Babe's pranks, got some of his own back by ribbing the Babe. Luckily, Perfect Records recorded the sketch on a 78 RPM record—it's "the only known commercial recording of the two of them together," noted Bill Francis in "At Home on the Road," an article for the National Baseball Hall of Fame. During the sketch, in response to Gehrig's teasing about his notoriously fast driving, Babe retorted, "I found a way out of it. When a policeman stops me, I autograph the car and give it to him as a souvenir."

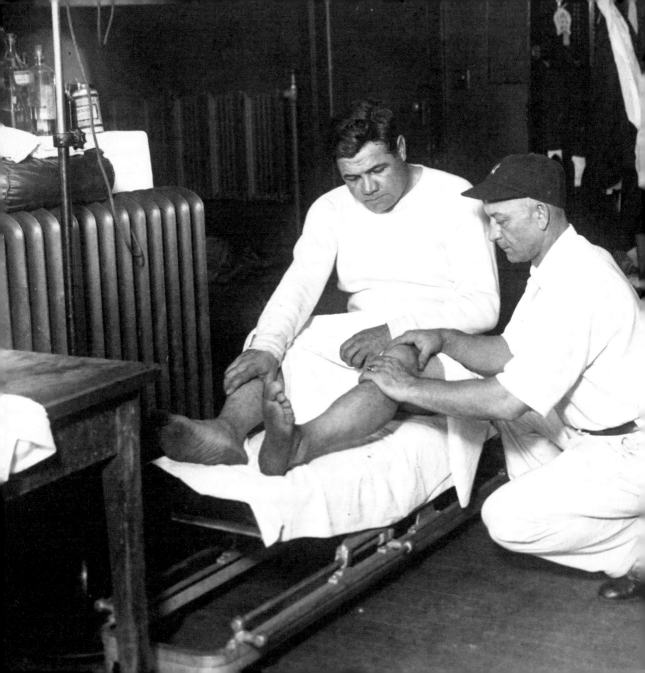

"YOU JUST CAN'T BEAT THE PERSON WHO NEVER GIVES UP."

"He ran with little mincing steps on thin legs, these delicate ankles, and he minced his way as though he were a dancer . . . doffing his cap left and right, bowing and waving to everybody and disappearing into the dugout."
—Studs Turkle

Babe getting checked out by a trainer in the Yankees' locker room, circa 1930.

"PICK OUT A GOOD
ONE AND SOCK IT!"

Post-1924 season, the Babe, Bob Meusel, and a cobbled together "All-Star" team set off on a two-week, 8,500-plus mile West Coast Barnstorming Tour with stops in fifteen cities, including Kansas City, Seattle, Portland, San Francisco, and Los Angeles, as well as this unscheduled stop in Dunsmuir. Off-field, Babe gave twenty-two speeches, headed four parades, refereed boxing bouts, visited eighteen hospitals and orphanages, and autographed nearly five thousand baseballs. On field, he played in fifteen games—against all comers—during which he pounded out seventeen home runs and set longest ball records in five ballparks. The longest of long, set in orbit during a seven-inning game in Dunsmuir Ball Park, flew 604 feet-a surveyor measured it!

Dunsmuir, California, October 24, 1924. Babe posing with members of the Mt. Shasta Girl's Baseball Team and a postcard of him poised to bat in Dunsmuir Ball Park (which is still in use). Bob Meusel is beside the dugout.

"DON'T BE AFRAID TO TAKE ADVICE. THERE'S ALWAYS SOMETHING NEW TO LEARN."

"Shoeless" Joe Jackson (on the right) looking over one of Babe's bats, circa 1920. The Babe freely admitted he copied his batting style from heavy hitter Joe Jackson, who earned the nickname "Shoeless" when he played one early game in socks because his new baseball cleats were hurting his feet. "I thought he [Shoeless Joe] was the greatest hitter I had ever seen, the greatest natural hitter I ever saw," Babe explained in *Joe Jackson: A Biography* by Kelly Boyer Sagerte. "He's the guy who made me a hitter."

Jackson described his hitting technique in an interview with Furman Bisher for *Sports Magazine*: "I used to draw a line three inches from the plate every time I came to bat. I drew a right angle line at the end of it, right next to the catcher, and put my left foot on it exactly three inches from home plate."

"IT'S WELL TO REMEMBER ALWAYS: YOU DON'T HAVE TO SWING."

"Babe is so weary of walking that he'll try anything to make the opposition pitch to him. Someday, we expect to see him go to bat with the stick in his teeth."
—*The New York Daily News*, August 1, 1923, in response to Babe batting right-handed

Babe waits for the pitch during one of the twenty-eight games he played with the Boston Braves in 1935. When he retired, Babe Ruth was the MLB official "Walk King." After having led the American League in BBs for eleven seasons, he ended his MLB career with 2,062 BBs, a record that stood until Rickey Henderson took over the title in 2001. In *The Big Bam: The Life and Times of Babe Ruth*, Leigh Montville noted that all those walks Babe took to first base added up to about thirty-four miles.

BABE IN BOSTON AND FULL OF BEANS

"The Babe pitched and won the first big-league game he ever saw, a distinction few major leaguers can claim."
—Sportswriter Tom Meany

On July 10, 1914, Babe boarded another train, this time a red-eye bound for Boston. The next afternoon, less than five months after leaving St. Mary's, Babe Ruth attended, *and played in*, his first-ever major league baseball game, as a starting pitcher for the Boston Red Sox. The Babe pitched seven innings against the Cleveland Naps, the worst team in the league at 26–49. Thanks to a save by Dutch Leonard, the game ended 4–3. Rookie Ruth notched his first MLB win.

"[Ruth] proved a natural ballplayer and went through his act like a veteran of many wars.
He has a natural delivery, fine control and a curve ball that bothers the batsmen."
—*The Boston Globe*

Earlier that day, fresh off the overnight train, Babe and teammate Ernie Shore headed straight for Landers Coffee Shop. Did Babe enjoy the huge breakfast he wolfed down? No telling. But there was something about that meal he couldn't forget: the charming sixteen-year-old waitress named Helen Woodford. Helen must have liked what he was dishing out, too, for they quickly became an item.

"George was six-foot-two, and weighed 198 pounds, all of it muscle. He had a slim waist, huge biceps, no self-discipline, and not much education—not so very different from a lot of other nineteen-year-old would-be ball players. Except for two things: he could eat more than anyone else, and he could hit a baseball further."
—Harry Hooper

Babe got another chance as starting pitcher the following week, this time against Detroit, but he blew it. After giving up two runs on three hits and a walk in the first three innings, he was pulled from the game. He did manage to strike out one batter but, tit-for-tat, in his only chance at bat, he struck out. The 2–5 loss dulled the shine on the new kid for Sox catcher-manager Bill Carrigan. Babe spent the next few weeks riding the bench and being razzed by teammates—the polar opposite of his experience with the Orioles and at St. Mary's. He felt the chill and didn't like it one bit. "The Red Sox wanted no part of me, a busher," Babe told biographer Norman L. Macht.

"I came up a southpaw pitcher and pitchers aren't supposed to hit—or to clutter up the batter's box . . . I saw no reason why I shouldn't take my licks. I'd get them usually, but there were times I'd go to my locker and find my bat sawed in half."
—Babe Ruth to Grantland Rice in *The Tumult and the Shouting*

On August 18, a little over a month after coming to the majors, Babe was shipped off to the minor leagues. Babe waved "so long" to Helen, Boston, and the Red Sox—but it was not goodbye.

Rhode Island's Providence Grays were first in the International League, in a three-way race for the pennant. One of the three was Babe's former team, the Baltimore Orioles. If the Grays were worried Babe might be more blow than show, they didn't worry long. The first chance he got, August 22, Babe wowed them.

"Babe Ruth appears to have gotten in on the ground floor with the fans as a result of his baffling southpaw brand of pitching and his ability to give the horse-hide vigorous punishment with the wagon tongue."
—*The Providence Journal*

Indeed, the Grays went on to win the 1914 International League Pennant, their first since 1905. Later it was reported that Sox manager Bill Carrigan hadn't sent Ruth down because he was too green. He'd been sent to Providence to help the Grays win the pennant. The rookie pitcher pulled his weight and then some; he went 23–8 to finish second in wins in the League. Mission accomplished, Babe returned to Boston and the Big Leagues.

On October 2, Babe got the chance to redeem himself with the Red Sox and he took it. In a home game against the Yankees, he pitched a win and made his first-ever major league hit, a double.

"Ex-Gray Pitches Fine Ball in Contest With Yankees."
—*The Providence Journal*

And he got the girl! After the season ended, on October 17, 1914, George Herman Ruth and Helen Woodford were married. The newlyweds spent the winter in Pigtown, Babe's old Baltimore neighborhood. It was the first time since his mother died that Babe had been back for any length of time. It was the first time he'd spent any real time with his father, sister, and other relatives too. With the turn of the year to 1915, Babe was riding high and raring to go when he reported for spring training.

Although no one realized it at the time, a new era in baseball launched on May 6, 1915. In a match against the Yankees at the Polo Grounds, top of the third inning, with nothing on the scoreboard and no one on base, George Herman Ruth stepped up to the plate against Yankees right-hander Jack Warhop. It was only the Babe's eighteenth time at bat in the MLB. While he'd had a couple of hits, no one expected much from the southpaw pitcher. Getting on base was the most anyone hoped for—from any player for that matter. After all, this was still the Deadball Era.

Deadball humbug! Babe sent the first ball that Warhop served flying "with a sound that made the 8,000 in attendance gasp," reporters noted.

"Ruth knocked the slant out of one of Jack Warhop's underhanded subterfuges and put the baseball in the right field stands for a home run."
—Damon Runyan, *New York American*

As surprising—and thrilling—as Babe's rocket into the right field grandstands was, it was shocking too, and so unexpected that sportswriter Wilmot Giffin noted how it was practically an insult to the Yankees' pitcher.

Portentous as it was, the homer didn't get much press in the next day's paper. Had they known it was number one of 714, it might have . . . or maybe not. The next day—May 7, 1915—the *Lusitania*, an American steamship, was torpedoed and sunk by a German submarine.

In 1915, Babe Ruth's first complete MLB season, the lefty pitcher won eighteen games and lost eight, batted .315, racked up four home runs, and earned his first World Series Championship (although he did not pitch in the Series). Along with a bonus check and a gold medallion with a baseball-shaped diamond center. (The World Series Championship ring tradition began in 1922.) He kept the medallion but spent his bonus on a saloon for his father.

Just in case anyone worried his starter season was a fluke, Babe bested his 1915 performance the following year. He won twenty-three games and posted a league-leading 1.75 ERA in 1916. He also threw nine shutouts—an American League southpaw pitching record. (That record was tied on September 24, 1978, by the Yankees' Ron Guidry, but has yet to be bested.) In Game Two of the 1916 World Series, the Babe pitched all fourteen innings of the longest World Series game ever played at the time—thirteen of them scoreless—to beat the Brooklyn Dodgers 2–1. He and his teammates took home another World Series Championship when the Sox won the series four games to one.

While on the Red Sox, the Babe pitched in and won three World Series games, the one in 1916 and two in 1918. During the 1918 series, he pitched twenty-nine 2/3 innings without giving up a run (breaking Christy Mathewson's record of twenty-eight 1/3 innings). Babe's record for scoreless innings in the World Series stood for forty-three years. Whitey Ford broke it in 1961 with thirty-three 1/3 scoreless innings. Red Sox ticket sales in 1917 proved what ticket sales in the two previous seasons had begun to show: As good as the fastball-throwing southpaw was on the mound, Babe the hitter was even better for the box office. Attendance soared on days the Babe was playing. Fans wanted to watch the Kid of Crash wield his bat. It wasn't so much about home runs yet—he only made two in 1917 with fourteen RBI—it was his ferocious all-or-nothing swing. After one game when Babe connected five times for three doubles and a triple, team captain Harry Hooper said as much to Sox manager Ed Barrow.

"We think the fans come out to see Ruth hit, so why not put him in the outfield every day?"
—Harry Hooper

Barrow ignored Hooper, claiming he'd be "the laughingstock of the league if I took the best pitcher in the league and put him in the outfield." He ignored Babe, who was itching for more playing time too.

"I like to pitch. But my main objection is that pitching keeps you out of so many games. I like to be in there every day."
—Babe Ruth in The Big Bam: The Life and Times of Babe Ruth by Leigh Montville

In 1918, with "the Great War," World War I, raging in Europe, baseball news came as welcome relief from the worries of war for readers, as well as to those serving abroad. An estimated 38 percent of major league players were serving in the military. Action and high drama like Babe brought to the game was just the diversion they wanted.

What baseball fans wanted, they got, and then some! During the Red Sox spring training in Hot Springs on St. Patrick's Day, Babe hit what's been called the "Home Run that Changed Everything"—baseball's first five-hundred-foot-plus drive from Whittington Park to the Alligator Farm. (According to the Historic Baseball Trail records, 573 feet to be exact!)

"Before the echo of the crash had died away the horsehide had dropped somewhere in the vicinity of South Hot Springs . . . The sphere cleared the fence by about 200 feet and dropped in the pond beside the Alligator Farm, while the spectators yelled with amazement."
—Paul Shannon, "Ruth Smashes Up Hopes of Dodgers," Boston Post, March 25, 1918

A few days later, to the delight of troops at Camp Pike, an Army training center on the other side of the state, Babe launched five homers during a hitting exhibition. And the hits just kept on coming!

Despite pressure from Hooper, Ruth, and fans, the 1918 season was underway before Red Sox management—namely Ed Barrow—started thinking with its pockets, and maybe only then because the team's regular first baseman injured his finger. On May 6, 1918, the Babe took over for Dick Hoblitzel. The next game, Babe started at first and in later games moved to the outfield.

During the last six weeks of the 1918 season, the Babe pitched one day, played outfield for the next three games, then pitched, then played outfield three games, and so on—pitching, playing, and hitting every game. The grueling schedule, that would have sent most other players crawling to the locker room, energized Babe.

One of the Fenway Park peanut vendors, Tom Foley, who was fourteen in 1918, recalled how Babe would arrive at Fenway Park early Saturday mornings to help the vendors bag peanuts, all the while joking and laughing and telling them to "be good boys and to play baseball."

"Babe Ruth was an angel to us. We'd all race to see who could bag the most [peanuts] and every once in a while, he'd flip a dollar bill across the table. Some kid would grab it and be thrilled . . . He thought that if we worked hard enough, we could be as good as he was. But we knew better than that. He'd stay about an hour. When we finished, he'd pull out a $20 bill and throw it on the table and say 'Have a good time, kids.'"
—Tom Foley to Allan Wood in "Someone Can Recall Red Sox Title," *Baseball America*, 1997

Slugger Babe was in every newspaper and on everyone's mind. Along with wanting to know if Babe hit and how far, everyone wanted to know what kind of stick he was using to blast such longballs. Hillerich & Bradsby, manufacturers of the Louisville Slugger, knew what having Babe's endorsement on a bat could do for sales. They had made a deal with "The Flying Dutchman" Honus Wagner, in 1905, to produce his signature bat—perhaps the first successful sports marketing effort—and it had paid off nicely. On July 9, 1918, Babe signed an agreement giving Hillerich & Bradsby the rights to make baseball bats with a copy of his signature on the barrel, for which he was paid $100. He didn't just sign the agreement letter; he signed it six times (so Hillerich & Bradsby could accurately reproduce his signature). More than one hundred years later, Babe Ruth's signature Louisville Slugger bats are still big sellers.

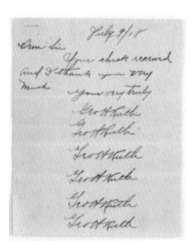

Years after they'd both retired, "The Georgia Peach," Ty Cobb—considered by many to be the "best all-around baseball player that ever lived"—noted the key to Babe Ruth's success as a hitter came from being free to "experiment at the plate" in those first seasons as a pitcher.

"He didn't have to get a piece of the ball. He didn't have to protect the plate the way a regular batter was expected to. No one cares much if the pitcher strikes out or looks bad at bat, so Ruth could take that big swing. If he missed, it didn't matter. And when he didn't miss, the ball went a long way. As time went on, he learned more and more about how to control that big swing and put the wood on the ball. By the time he became a full-time outfielder, he was ready." —Ty Cobb

If Cobb's theory is correct, then Babe's experimenting paid off. In 1919, Babe Ruth's last season with the Red Sox, he led the American League with 113 RBI and twenty-nine homers. (Altogether the rest of the team only hit four home runs.)

Over the course of his twenty-two-season MLB career—including three as a full-time pitcher—Babe Ruth hit 714 home runs in 3,965 fewer at-bats than Hank Aaron, who finished a twenty-three-year career with 755 home runs. If Babe Ruth had begun his career in the daily lineup rather than starting his career in the pitching rotation, who knows how many more homers he might have racked up.

"Johnny Honig sat on the wall
Babe Ruth clouted the ball.
All Dunn's players and the groundskeeper's men
Couldn't find the ball again."
—C. Starr Matthews, *The Baltimore Sun*, April 19, 1919

Even so, the 1919 season was a total flop for the Red Sox, who finished sixth in the American League—twenty 1/2 games behind the Chicago White Sox. It was an even bigger flop for Harry Frazee, the Red Sox owner, who was in financial trouble. Conversely, Babe finished the season on top of the heap. In 432 at-bats, the Colossus of Clout racked up 139 hits—twenty-nine of them home runs, seventy-five of them extra-base hits—and scored 103 runs (more than any other player in the league).

At the start of the 1919 season, the Babe had signed a three-year $30,000 contract to play for the Red Sox. But then he'd started knocking out homers. By season's end, he wanted a new contract for double the money, and he let everyone know it.

"You can say for me . . . that I will not play with the Red Sox unless I get $20,000. You may think that sounds like a pipe dream, but it is the truth. I feel that I made a bad move last year when I signed a three-year contract to play for $30,000. The Boston club realized much on my value and I think that I am entitled to twice as much as my contract calls for."
—Babe Ruth, *The Boston Globe*, October 24, 1919

For Harry Frazee, whose heart and interest lay more in other ventures than it did in baseball—namely Broadway shows—there was a simple two-word solution to his money woes: Sell Babe.

"I do not wish to detract one iota from Ruth's ability as a ballplayer nor from his value as an attraction, but there is no getting away from the fact that despite his 29 home runs, the Red Sox finished sixth in the race last season . . . What the Boston fans want, I take it, and what I want because they want it, is a winning team, rather than a one-man team which finishes in sixth place."
—Harry Frazee

As luck would have it, Frazee's buddy, the New York Yankees' co-owner Jacob Ruppert was buying. At the press conference announcing Babe's acquisition, Ruppert refused to confirm or deny the terms of the agreement.

"I can say positively, however, that it is by far the biggest price ever paid for a ballplayer. Ruth was considered a champion of all champions, and, as such, deserving of an opportunity to shine before the sport lovers of the greatest metropolis of the world."
—Jacob Ruppert

After the sale, the Red Sox wouldn't win another World Series until 2004—eighty-six seasons—the second-longest dry spell in MLB history. (The Chicago Cubs 108-season drought was the longest). Boston fans called the losing streak the "Curse of the Bambino," but selling Babe was only partly to blame. Between December 1919 and July 1923, when, having gutted the team, Frazee sold the Red Sox altogether, he lost manager Ed Barrow and seventeen players to the Yankees, most spectacularly, Babe Ruth. *The New York Times* January 6, 1920, headlines read:

YANKS BUY BABE RUTH FOR $125,000

Highest Purchase Price in Baseball History Paid for Game's Greatest Slugger.

WILL GET NEW CONTRACT

Miller Huggins Is Now in California to Sign Home-Run King at Large Salary.

SLATED FOR RIGHT FIELD

Acquisition of Noted Batsman Gives New York Club the Hard-Hitting Outfielder Long Desired.

Frazee sold Babe Ruth's contract to the New York Yankees for $125,000 in cash plus a $300,000 loan, with Fenway Park as collateral.

That $125,000—more than $2.5 million in today's dollars—was the highest price ever paid for a player to date. On January 6, 1920, *The New York Times* also published this list of popular players' salaries:

Largest Sums on Record for Purchase of Ball Players

Babe Ruth, Boston to Yankees.. ....$125,000
Tris Speaker, Boston to Cleveland *50,000
Eddie Collins, Athletics to Chicago 50,000
Carl Mays, Boston to Yankees *40,000
Art Nehf, Boston to Giants.. *40,000
Frank Baker, Athletics to Yankees 37,500
Joe Jackson, Cleveland to Chicago *31,500
Benny Kauff, Feds to Giants. 30,000
Lee Magee, Feds to Yankees. 22,500
Strunk, Schang, and Bush, Athletics to Boston........ *60,000
Alexander and Killefer, Phillies to Chicago............ *55,000
*And players.

At the press conference announcing the deal, Jacob Ruppert laid out plans for the Yankees in no uncertain terms:

"It is not only our intention, but a strong life purpose, moreover, to give the loyal American League fans of greater New York an opportunity to root for our team in a World's Series. We are going to give them a Pennant winner, no matter what the cost. I think the addition of Ruth to our forces should help greatly along those general lines."
—*The New York Times*, January 5, 1920

How Babe's future teammates felt about making room for him in the dugout was summed up best by Bob Shawkey, one of the Yankees' pitchers:

"Gee, I'm glad that guy's not going to hit against me anymore. You take your life in your hands every time you step up against him. You just throw up anything that happens to come into your head, with a prayer, and duck for your life with the pitch."
—Bob Shawkey

"IT ONLY TAKES ONE."

"It's going! Babe Ruth connects and here it goes! The ball is going, going, going—high into the center-field stands, into the scoreboard! And it's a home run! It's gone! Whoopee! Listen to that crowd!"
— NBC announcer Tom Manning, October 1, 1932

"The Bambino hit two homers during the day, each of them a record breaker, and on the occasion of his second round-tripper even went so far as to call his shot. He also cross-fired gags with hecklers on the Cub bench to draw rounds of laughs . . . in the fifth with the Cubs riding him unmercifully from the bench, Ruth pointed to center field and punched a screaming liner to a spot where no ball had been hit before."
—Joe Williams, *The New York World-Telegram*

"Do I believe he really called it? Yes Sir. I was there; I saw it. I don't care what anybody says. He did it."
—Yankees third-baseman Joe Sewell to Donald Honig, *The October Heroes*

Game Three of the 1932 World Series against the Chicago Cubs, held on October 1, 1932, at Wrigley Field. Babe's "Called Shot" was captured on a sixteen-millimeter home movie camera taken by spectator Matt Kandle Sr.

In the fifth inning, with the score tied 4–4, Babe stepped up to the plate. Charlie Root's first pitch was a strike, followed by two balls and strike two. Babe, who had already scored once that game, was being heckled by Chicago fans and players—and giving back as good as he got. In the midst of the melee, the Cubs' catcher, Gabby Hartnett, and Little Ray Kelly, Ruth's mascot, both heard Babe holler to Root, "It only takes one." That's when the Babe pointed toward centerfield and blasted the next pitch. Decades later, the debate over whether Babe targeted his hit or just got lucky continues. "Called Shot" or not, that was Babe Ruth's second homer of the day and the NY Yankees won the Series in a four-game sweep.

"ALL FORMS OF ATHLETICS DEPEND ON TIMING. IT'S THE SECRET OF GOLF AND HANDBALL AND TENNIS. IT'S THE SECRET OF BOXING, AND IT'S THE SECRET OF FOOTBALL OFFENSE."

"Both Carry a Mighty Wallop." April 13, 1933, heavyweight boxing champ Jack Dempsey kicked off the season opener at Yankee Stadium by presenting Babe Ruth with a humongous bat. Throughout the 1920s, Dempsey and Ruth shared the title of the most popular athlete in America, if not the world. Their popularity—and similarities—inspired ten-year-old John Lardner, sportswriter Ring Lardner's son, to compare the two:

Babe Ruth and Old Jack Dempsey
Both Sultans of Swat
One hits where other people are—
The other hits where they're not.
—John Lardner

This quatrain originally appeared in Franklin Pierce Adams's syndicated column, "The Conning Tower."

"I HEAR THE CHEERS WHEN THEY ROARED AND THE JEERS WHEN THEY ECHOED."

"You can't forget that face."
—Ray Robinson

"He had the face of a happy catcher's mitt."
—Donald Honig

"Who has ever looked like him since Babe Ruth? Try to think of someone who looked like him. It's like he was created for this role that he was given, and he played it to the hills."
—Bill Gleason

In a time when sketches rather than photographs were the norm, Babe's features were so distinct, even the poorest artist could draw a fair likeness of him.

93

"A LOT OF THINGS WHICH MAY NOT PLEASE THE FOLKS IN THE STANDS ARE MIGHTY GOOD BASEBALL ALL THE SAME."

"I remember one time we were playing the White Sox in Boston in 1919, and he hit a home run off Lefty Williams over the left-field fence in the ninth inning and won the game. It was majestic. It soared. We watched it and wondered, 'How can a guy hit a ball like that.'"
—Waite Hoyt to Leigh Montville in *The Big Bam: The Life and Times of Babe Ruth*

The Babe and Hall of Fame pitcher Waite "Schoolboy" Hoyt were teammates for ten full seasons, first as Red Sox then as Yankees.

"IT IS TIMING WHICH, MORE THAN ANY ONE THING, IS THE SECRET OF REAL HITTING."

"The tests revealed that Ruth is 90 per cent efficient compared with a human average of 60 percent . . . his eyes are about 12 per cent faster than those of the ordinary man . . . his nerves are steadier than those of 499 out of 500 persons. That in attention and quickness of perception he rated one and a half times the human average. That in intelligence, as demonstrated by quickness and accuracy of understanding, he is approximately 10 per cent above normal."
—Hugh Fullerton, *Popular Science Monthly*, October 1921

As shown in these diagrams of Babe hitting, published in **The Richmond Times Dispatch** on July 18, 1920, everyone wanted to know the secret of his superpower. One hot August afternoon in 1920, sportswriter Hugh Fullerton talked Babe into having his coordination tested at the Columbia University Psychological Research Lab. Psychologists Albert Johanson and Joseph Holmes put Babe through three hours of testing, which included inserting a stylus into holes on a board, tapping a metal plate as fast as possible, identifying letters, counting dots flashing before his eyes, and swinging a bat at a suspended ball to record his speed and power—all after Babe had already played a nine-inning game.

Testing Babe Ruth for Quickness of Eye, Brain and Muscle

Ruth was told to press the telegraph-key when a light flashed on the board before him. Results showed that his muscles responded to the eye-and-brain impulse more than one tenth quicker than do those of the average person. Scientists say this is one reason why he can follow a sharp breaking curve with his bat and hit the ball fair enough to drive it far over the fence

Babe Ruth holds his breath when he bats. For that reason he is not getting the maximum force into his batting. This fact was recorded by the pneumatic tube around his chest that measured his breathing

"I CONSIDER MYSELF TO BE THE MOST ABSURDLY FORTUNATE GUY TO HAVE SLID INTO THE 20TH CENTURY SAFE."

"He was so grateful to have an honest-to-goodness family, due to losing his mother at such a young age. Momma loved him and so did Gene and Hubert [Claire's brothers]. He thought the world of all of them. It's not every day that someone would be willing to bring in a whole family like that. Maybe a mother-in-law, but also two brothers? But he just loved it."
—Julia Ruth Stevens, *Babe Ruth: Remembering the Bambino in Stories, Photos, and Memorabilia*

Babe celebrating his 39th (what he later learned was actually his 38th) birthday with his family (left–right) Julia, Dorothy, and Claire, 1933.

"YESTERDAY'S HOME RUNS
DON'T WIN TODAY'S GAMES."

In the fall of 1934, the "All American" All-Stars embarked on an eighteen-game barnstorming tour of Japan, organized by Connie Mack with Matsutaro Shoriki, founder of Japanese professional baseball. Along with the twelve-city tour in Japan, where they played against Japan's Big-Six University teams, the All-Stars played in Vancouver, Hawaii, China, and the Philippines. Babe served as team manager, no easy task considering the complicated logistics, cultural differences, travel glitches, and personalities. Jimmie Foxx said Babe managed the tour as though it were the World Series, which was okay by him.

The All-Americans team included fourteen players from the American League: Babe Ruth, Lou Gehrig, Lefty Gomez, Joe Cascarella, Jimmie Foxx, Eric McNair, Bing Miller, Frankie Hayes, Harold "Rabbit" Warstler, Charlie Gehringer, Earl Averill, Clint Brown, Earl Whitehill, and Moe Berg, along with Lefty O'Doul coaching and umpire John Quinn.

"I'VE HEARD PEOPLE SAY THAT THE TROUBLE WITH THE WORLD IS THAT WE HAVEN'T ENOUGH GREAT LEADERS. I THINK WE HAVEN'T ENOUGH GREAT FOLLOWERS."

"The Japanese were literally crazy about baseball . . . Babe Ruth was their idol."
—Connie Mack

At every stop on the Japan Goodwill Tour, the All-Americans were greeted by hundreds of thousands of cheering fans. "It seemed like all Tokyo was out, waving and yelling. We could hardly get our cars through, the streets were so jammed," Charlie Gehringer recalled. Babe mostly played first base on the tour. In one game he played seven positions. Every time he came up to bat the fans rose to their feet cheering and waving American and Japanese flags. Babe hit two homers in Sendai, during the fourth game of the tour. Babe wowed the crowd by hitting a homer in almost every game—with thirteen in the last thirteen games.

"HOW'S ABOUT A LITTLE NOISE? HOW DO YOU EXPECT A MAN TO PUNT."

"The first rule of golf which says, 'make your swing easy and natural, and don't press,' could well be named as the first rule of pitching too."
—Babe Ruth

Babe golfing in Seattle, November 24, 1926.

For Babe—who took up golf shortly after turning pro—golf and baseball went hand in hand. In fact, reporters often compared his batting style to a golf swing. As his daughter Julia Ruth Stevens noted, "If he wasn't so good at baseball I think he would have wanted to become a professional golfer."

For nine seasons, beginning in 1915 as a rookie pitcher, Babe trained in Hot Springs, Arkansas, first during spring training with the Red Sox and then after to shape up pre-spring training with the Yankees. To get in shape, along with hiking the mountains and taking steam baths, Babe golfed. He was a regular at Hot Springs Country Club where he'd often play thirty-six holes a day, sometimes fifty-four.

"WHO IS RICHER? THE MAN WHO IS SEEN, BUT CANNOT SEE? OR THE MAN WHO IS NOT BEING SEEN, BUT CAN SEE?"

"The Yanks are winning a laugher, 16–5, when a dog wanders onto left field in the 9th inning. Babe Ruth briefly plays with the pup, then tosses his mitt to chase it away. The dog promptly grabs the mitt and takes off at the same moment that Sox rookie pitcher Paul Castner lofts a fly to left. Babe casually catches the fly bare handed."
—*Chicago Sun Times*, August 20, 1923, reprinted August 20, 2015

Human fans regularly wandered onto the field to meet Babe, but August 20, 1923, was a dog's day in Comiskey Park. (This photo of Babe hugging a dog named Hazel accompanied Dan Cahill's recount of the event for the *Chicago Sun Times*, but it's a different dog, a different day.)

BABE IN THE BIG APPLE

"New York of 1920 was built for him. He was a muscle man coming to a muscle city in a muscle time."
—Leigh Montville, *The Big Bam: The Life and Times of Babe Ruth*

Babe's trade to the New York Yankees was the best thing that could have happened to him personally and professionally. The city of Boston was too buttoned up for a man-boy who not only didn't mind his manners but was having far too much fun to care what proper manners were. In contrast, New York City in the 1920s was happening! It was the commercial, industrial, cultural center of the country—arguably the world—wild and wide open.

Ironically, while Boston the city was perhaps too small for the man and legend "Bunyan" Babe was becoming, Boston the team was too big. The Red Sox were a talent powerhouse ("were" being the operative word here)—they didn't **need** him. The Yankees did. When Babe swapped his Boston red socks for New York's navy, he traded one of MLB's best teams for one of the worst. Beginning with the first modern World Series in 1903, the Red Sox had won five of fifteen played. In contrast, not only had the Yankees never made it into the World Series, but most seasons they finished in the bottom half of the league.

Yankees' owners Jacob Ruppert, Jr. and Tillinghast L'Hommedieu "Cap" Huston—the "Two Colonels" as they came to be called—were as different as could be. Huston was a perfectionist engineer; Ruppert a social gadabout. But where the Yankees were concerned, they shared a few very important traits: they were both ferociously competitive, they both loved baseball, they both had means (although Cap's pockets weren't as deep as Ruppert's), and they both wanted the Yankees to win. How to make that happen was another thing.

After their first manager, Wild Bill Donovan, didn't work out, the Two Colonels haggled over who should replace him. Finally, Ruppert took matters into his own hands. Taking advantage of Huston's absence serving in World War I, Ruppert hired the Cardinal's manager, Miller Huggins. (Ruppert's hiring of Huggins remained a source of contention between the two owners until Huston finally sold his share of the team to Ruppert in 1922.) Miller Huggins, "Hug," was a tiny but mighty second-baseman-turned-manager and licensed lawyer, with, as sportswriter Hyatt Daab put it, no more personality "than a stark old oak tree against a gray winter sky" ("Timely News and Views in the World of Sport," *Evening Telegram*, October 26, 1920). Miller Huggins unapologetically professed his whole life centered around one thing:

"I fell in love . . . the object of my love, though, was no lady. It was baseball."
—Miller Huggins, "How I Got That Way," *New York Evening Post*, October 2, 1926

From October 1917, when Miller Huggins signed with the Yankees, until his untimely death from blood poisoning in 1929, his business was Yankees' baseball. Jacob Ruppert later said he believed hiring Huggins, who led the team to six AL pennants and three World Series wins, was the "first and most important step in turning the Yankees from also-rans into champions" ("The Colonel and Hug: The Odd Couple . . . Not Really" by Steve Steinberg and Lyle Spatz, *Baseball Research Journal*, Fall 2015).

Miller Huggins had as much to do with Babe Ruth joining the Yankees as anyone. Well aware of Babe's already established reputation as a "problem" player—which included childish tantrums, arguing with management, and refusing to follow rules—Huggins believed Babe was the lynchpin to building the team. So much so that, while negotiations were underway, Huggins went to California to convince Babe to sign with the team.

"The Yankees probably would have become the fabulous success they are now without the Babe, but, I'm certain, the road to the top would have been much longer and much less exciting."
—Grantland Rice, *Sport* magazine, September 1951

True to form, just before the Yankees' departure for 1920 Spring Training in Jacksonville, Florida, the Kid of Crash blew into town. Full of himself, and full of beans, Babe strutted into the train station, tanned, loud, dressed to the nines, and followed by a porter pulling a cart loaded with suitcases, brand-new golf clubs, and a parade of fans. At twenty-five, he was the most expensive player in baseball, and for good reason.

"Ruth's crowning batting accomplishment came at the Polo Grounds last fall when he hammered one of the longest hits ever seen in Harlem over the right field grandstand for his twenty-eighth home run, smashing the home record of twenty-seven, made by Ed Williamson way back in 1884."
—*The New York Times*, January 6, 1920

On the first day in Jacksonville, March 1, after practice, Babe opted to play golf. According to news reports, dressed in silks and flannels, he threw his club into the air to stop a golf ball midflight—and did! Meanwhile, with the $125,000 question hanging in the air, votes were out on whether the Yankees were shrewd or suckers. Everyone in the baseball world, especially sportswriters, tracked Babe's every move.

On March 19, Babe gave them something to write about, and then some. He blasted his first big hit since the start of spring training. It was a long ball over the centerfield fence.

"Yes, sir, clean, over, right over. My what a swat it was.
My! My! My! My! My! My! My! My! My! My! My! My! My! My! My! My! My! Plumb over."
—Sportswriter Damon Runyon, *New York American*

In *The Big Bam: The Life and Times of Babe Ruth*, Leigh Montville noted how the sportswriters were so giddy over how far Babe's hit had gone, they "hustled out with a tape measure and figured the ball had traveled 478 feet. The fence was 428 feet, and the ball had traveled 50 feet more."

Opening game of the 1920 season, April 14, Babe had a bit of the stuffing knocked out of him when he dropped a fly ball that cost the Yankees the game. The next game, he struck out three times—once with the bases loaded. And for the next few weeks, he didn't perform any better. As fast as the Bay of Fundy tides, opinions about him changed. Suddenly everyone was saying the critics, who doubted anyone would ever hit as many home runs as he had in 1919, were correct.

Finally on May 1, 1920, the Babe hit his first homer as a Yankee. Adding injury to the already insulted Red Sox fans, the homer was served up by his former Sox teammate Herb Pennock. The "sockdolager" sailed over the right grandstand roof and into the street.

The next day Babe blasted another one. Not so high but just as spectacularly. The delighted crowd went wild, programs and hats rained down like confetti, and fans swarmed the field. ***That did it!*** Once in the swing of it, the Babe never looked back. In the May 11 game, he went three-for-three with a walk. Two of those hits were home runs and one was a triple.

"Ruth's principle of batting is much the same as the principle of the golfer. He comes back slowly, keeps his eye on the ball and follows through. His very position at bat is intimidating to the pitcher. He places his feet in perfect position. He simply cannot step away from the pitch if he wants to. He can only step one way—in."
—*The New York Times*, January 6, 1920

Babe, "the Blunderbuss", came along at exactly the right time for baseball and for the country. Compared with today, 1920s America was still in the dark ages. Literally. Only 35 percent of the homes even had electricity. That meant no televisions and scant radios. Newspapers were people's primary source of news and entertainment. Every town and city had at least one paper; New York had thirteen. That was a lot of pages to fill, a lot of stories to tell. But not just any stories. Still wobbly after World War I, Americans wanted good news, fun news, exciting news. Bold Babe, Brash Babe, Baseball-basher Babe was all of that and more. As Babe Fever spread, sportswriters thumbed their thesauri thinking up new ways to describe his playing, and the legend grew.

"Babe was no ordinary man. He was not only the idol of the fans, he was superman to the ball players. He was their man, their guy. Ruth possessed a magnetism that was positively infectious. When he entered a clubhouse, or a room; when he appeared on a field—it was as if he was a whole parade."
—Waite Hoyt

Before the 1929 season, players didn't wear uniforms with numbers. It was hard to tell one player from the next on grainy newsprint, let alone from the back of the bleachers. Distinguishing features like Harry Wright's double-decker beard, Lou Gehrig's dimples, "King" Kelly's handlebar mustache, DiMaggio's nose, and Yogi Berra's "jughandle" ears helped players stand out on the field and in print. Maybe that's why Pitcher Bob Shawkey wore red sleeves under his uniform? Babe didn't need a mustache or red shirt; his large round face, broad nose, downturned eyes, and expressive mouth made him an instant standout.

"He had the most famous face in the world. If he appeared out of the grave today, everyone would know who he was."
—Sportswriter Ray Robinson in *USA Today Baseball Weekly*, August 12, 1998

In those days, sportswriters traveled with the baseball teams so they could be there to watch the game and write about it. Riding the same trains, staying in the same hotels, eating together, and especially the long train rides between cities in each other's company gave writers plenty of time to get to know the players and plenty to write about—if players were willing. Some players preferred to keep to themselves. But not the Babe.

"Babe always had time for the writers. After they exhausted every question about baseball, they would launch into other subjects: politics, women's rights, gambling, money, golf, traveling, cars, religion—you name it. Dad was never at a loss for words, whether he understood the question or not."
—Babe Ruth's daughter Dorothy Ruth Pirone

Babe's popularity was helped in part by a series of articles contracted by the **United News Service**. The series, originally published in August of 1920 and mostly ghostwritten in Babe's folksy banter, began with autobiographical accounts of Babe's childhood and his early days in the minors, the Red Sox, and the Yankees. The series was extended to include recaps of each of Babe's home runs, analysis of the AL Pennant race and the World Series. The articles, printed in newspapers everywhere, contributed to Babe Fever infecting the country and beyond.

"I put the old ball on ice for my forty-fourth this afternoon. I cracked one of Kerr's shots into my favorite spot, the right field stands and drove a man in ahead of me."
—Babe Ruth, New York, August 26, 1920, *Playing the Game: My Early Years in Baseball*

The puppeteer behind the syndicated article series was writer–cartoonist–former ad man–lawyer Christy Walsh, who, beginning with Babe, became baseball's first agent/manager. Walsh entered Babe's life either via a fire escape or by posing as a delivery guy and ala **Jerry McGuire** announced, "I want to represent you!"

Babe's prowess on the field had already rocketed him into sports stardom when Walsh came along. Hoping to capitalize on that success, he made a few side deals, including signing a movie contract and selling signature rights to Louisville Slugger, but Babe wanted more. When Walsh approached him about joining his fledgling ghost-writing syndicate, Babe said, "Yes!" And Babe kept saying "yes" to product endorse-ments, interviews, personal appearances . . . "yes," "yes," "yes." Thus, Walsh went from ghostwriting stories about Babe to managing Babe—professionally and personally.

Babe Fever was good for the Yankees. It was good for baseball period. And baseball needed all the **good** it could get in 1920. The season had opened under a cloud as rumors swirled that the 1919 World Series had been fixed. Then, on August 17, Cleveland Indian shortstop Ray Chapman died as the result of being hit in the head by one of Yankees' pitcher Carl May's fastballs. Already soured on the sport, by Septem-ber, when eight White Sox players (along with five gamblers) were indicted for taking bribes to throw the 1919 Series, many fans were ready to give up on baseball . . But not all baseball. And definitely not when it came to Babe Ruth. Nobody wanted to miss out on a chance to see the Babe in action.

September 24, 1920: Babe Hit His Hundredth Home Run

The "Mastodon of Mash" ended the 1920 season with fifty-four home runs. The St Louis Browns, **as a team**, came in second with fifty. Babe's 1920 slugging average percent-age of .847 set an MLB record that stood until 1926 when power hitter George "Mules" Suttles topped it with .877 in the Negro Leagues.

"Babe not only smashed all records, he has smashed the long-accepted system of things in the batting world and on the ruins of that system, he has erected another system, or rather lack of system, whose dominate quality is brute force."
—F.C. Lane, *Baseball Magazine*

The Yankees finished the 1920 season third in the League. But that was on the field. In the stands, the Yanks were tops. The Two Colonels' gamble had paid off. The 1920 Yankees were the first team in any sport to draw over a million spectators, more than double their 1919 gate. They broke attendance records in all six American League stadiums and drew the highest attendance by far of any team in the majors, including at the Polo Grounds where they surpassed attendance of the "other" home team—the New York Giants—by roughly 350,000 fans.

"The Black Sox threw the 1919 World Series and Carl Mays killed a player
with a pitch in 1920, but because of Babe, baseball thrived."
—Sportswriter Jim Cable, *Sport* magazine, December 1999

To the Giants, who had dominated New York baseball until then and also owned the Polo Grounds, the fan drain (brought about largely because of the Bambino) was personal and insulting. Until that season, the Yankees had been mere renters and, until Babe joined them, insignificant. The Giants' owner, Horace Stoneham, retaliated by evicting the Yankees. The Yankees would have to find a new place to play. (Stoneham eventually relented and extended the team's lease for another two years.)

By the time Babe joined the Yankees, he was full time in the outfield. But before switching to the outfield, Babe was the best southpaw pitcher around. Whether he would have stayed the course had he remained a pitcher remains a matter of debate. He did start four games and appeared in a fifth as a Yankee pitcher—just to shake things up—and won them all. A perfect 5–0 record. His contribution to the Yankees outfield speaks for itself.

"[Babe Ruth] deserves to be rated among the greatest outfielders of all time. He covers a wide territory, is sure death on fly balls and all the line drives he can get his hands on, plays ground balls that come to him as well as an infielder, and throws amazingly."
—Arthur Fletcher, Yankees third-base coach (1926–45), *New York Sun*, May 25, 1927

Which position Babe played didn't much matter to him. What mattered was that he played. That's what the fans wanted too. But not just playing—swinging away! So that's what the Yankees wanted. Along with Babe's 1921 contract, they offered him an incentive to aim for the sky—as if he needed it: $50 bucks for every home run.

"He had a violent swing. And if he missed, he'd cork screw in the batter's box
and wind up facing the grandstand. He looked like a beer keg on stilts."
—Sportswriter Stan Hochman, *Philadelphia Daily News*, August 1998

Whether it was the bonus or not, Babe didn't disappoint. The King of Swing had reporters working overtime trying to come up with new names to call his hits. He blasted, banged out, bashed, rocketed, smashed, slugged, and walloped homers. In June, he hit seven home runs in five days. And on September 15, 1921, Babe knocked out his fifty-fifth homer of the season, which broke his prior best.

"The Caliph of Crash, with the whiz of an ashen club, smoked number 55
in the first game of a doubleheader against the St. Louis Browns."
—*Los Angeles Times*, September 16, 1921

"Ruth's tremendous slash stood forth among all the drives of the dual affray like an antelope among ants, for it was the one of which most of the 30,000 onlookers had talked and dreamed for, lo, these many moons."
—William Enlivens Games, *The New York Times*, September 16, 1921

If there had been an MLB Most Valuable Player Award to win in 1921, the Babe would have won it. If there had been a presidential election in 1921, Babe could very well have won that too. An editorial in the **Los Angeles Times** declared Babe the nation's foremost hero, but then went on to say that if he were to run for president, "Popularity would defeat him; for to put him in the White House would be to take him out of baseball."

"You know about his year, 1921: .378 [BA], hit 59 home runs, scored 178 runs,
drove in 171 runs, got over 40 doubles, 16 triples, stole 16 bases. That was Babe Ruth."
—Bill Mazer, HBO *Babe Ruth* documentary

For the record, 1921 was the first and only time the Yankees offered Babe Ruth a home run bonus.

"Babe Ruth could hit a ball so hard, and so far, that it was sometimes impossible to believe your eyes. We used to absolutely marvel at his hits. Tremendous wallops. You can't imagine the balls he hit."
—Opposing pitcher and teammate Sad Sam Jones to Lawrence S. Ritter in *The Glory of Their Times*

Despite newspaper headlines, 1921 Yankees' baseball wasn't solely "the Babe Show." The roster was studded with stars: heavy hitters Bob Meusel and Frank "Home Run" Baker, Chick Fewster, Aaron Ward, and several former Red Sox, including catcher Wally Schang, Waite Hoyt, and submarine pitcher Carl Mays, who was infamous for having fatally struck Ray Chapman with a fastball the previous year.

The Yankees finished the 1921 season with a 98–55 record to win their first coveted American League pennant. Even though they lost the World Series to the Giants, the Yankees were on their way from being New York's "other team" to becoming its capital 'T' Team.

"Up to a couple of years ago, the Yanks were just the 'other New York team.' But the immense personal popularity of Babe Ruth and the dynamite in the rest of that Yankee batting order have made the Yanks popular with the element that loves the spectacular."
—Sid Mercer, *New York Evening Journal*, October 3, 1921

For Babe and Helen, 1921 was a personal highlight as well. The couple welcomed a daughter, Dorothy. Circumstances surrounding Dorothy's arrival were murky and the press had a field day trying to sort it out. Babe loved being part of a family and relished the time he spent with them, especially getaways to Home Plate Farm in Sudbury, Massachusetts, where they played at being farmers and, in turn, raised chickens, turkeys, and even dogs. Babe enjoyed being outdoors, hunting, fishing, country life in general, as did Helen. But Country Babe and City Babe were two very different people. Celebrity, living large, and being on the road presented many temptations. This was the Roaring Twenties! The Jazz Age! "The Era of Wonderful Nonsense," sportswriter Westbrook Pegler called it. After having spent his formative years "imprisoned" at St. Mary's, almost exclusively in the company of boys and men, Babe had erased "temperance" from his vocabulary.

"Dad never swallowed goldfish, hung from flagpoles or entered any dance marathons, all ingenious ways of having a 'good' time, but he probably did not miss out on much else. He lived life at breakneck speed, with no time to waste for red lights or slaps on the wrist."
—Dorothy Ruth Pirone

Come 1922, the Yankees' owners—mostly Ruppert—set their caps on building the Yankees their first official home field. Ed Barrow and Miller Huggins focused on continuing to build the team, which included adding former Red Sox Sad Sam Jones, Joe Bush, and Everett Scott to the roster. And Babe focused on being Babe: for better *and* worse. He started the season in the doghouse, er, dugout, along with teammate Bob Meusel, as punishment for defying MLB rules against World Series participants barnstorming. After six weeks of riding the bench, out of shape and out of sorts, Babe pretty much stayed in the doghouse. He missed games, threw tantrums, argued, caroused . . . disappointed off and on the field, where for the first time in four years, he failed to lead the league in home runs.

Despite Ruth, the Yankees finished 1922 with their second league championship. But as construction on Yankee Stadium continued—a project conceived and funded primarily because of the Babe's popularity—doubts about his future circulated.

Was baseball's superstar burning out? At a postseason baseball writers' dinner, New York state senator James J. Walker raked Babe over the coals for his 1922 performance while voicing everyone's doubts about the coming season:

> "Babe, are you going to once again let down those dirty-faced kids in the streets of America."
> —*The Big Bam: The Life and Times of Babe Ruth* by Leigh Montville

Walker's reprimand hit Babe hard. Even back at St. Mary's, he'd spent what little pocket money he was allowed to keep on candy for younger boys who didn't have any. He'd sign endless autographs, stop to play pickup ball with kids, and always took time to visit children in hospitals and orphanages. The idea that he would ever willingly "let down kids" was unfathomable.

> "Babe never once turned down a promise to go somewhere and visit some kids
> unless it was because he had a previous obligation to visit kids somewhere else."
> —Sportswriter Tom Meany

Right then, Babe vowed, "I'll go to the country and get in shape." Along with Helen and Dorothy, Babe skedaddled to Home Plate Farm, where he spent the fall and winter focused on clean living and getting fit. True to his word, by the time Yankee Stadium—the biggest, tallest, grandest baseball park of its time (the first to be called a "Stadium")—was ready, the Babe was ready too.

On April 18, 1923, prior to the opening day game in Yankee Stadium against the Boston Red Sox, Babe famously announced, "I'd give a year of my life if I can hit a home run in this first game in this new park." In the third inning, with two on and two outs, the chance came, and Babe took it:

"He fouled off Red Sox pitcher Howard Ehmke's first pitch, took a ball, hit another pitch foul, and watched ball two go by. Then Ehmke left a letter-high curveball over the plate that Ruth ripped several rows up into the bleachers for a three-run blast that gave the Yankees a 4–0 lead."
—"The Paying Colonels Draw Dividend When King George Whacks," *Boston Herald*, April 19, 1923

May 12, 1923, Babe Hit His Two Hundredth Career Home Run

Thus began a banner year!

The Yankees finished the regular season sixteen games ahead of the Detroit Tigers to win their third straight AL championship and finally bested the Giants—their now across-the-river rivals—four games to two to win the team's first-ever World Series title. As for Babe, anyone doubting why the Yankee Stadium was nicknamed "The House that Ruth Built" need only check the stats. Babe finished the season with forty-one home runs, 130 RBI, and a .393 batting average—a Yankees' single-season record that still stands—and led to him winning his only MVP Award. (No doubt he would have won more, but until the rules were changed in 1931, players were only eligible to win MVP once.)

The year 1923 was remarkable for the Yankees, as well as for Babe personally; midway through the season, Lou Gehrig joined the team. Gehrig was being lauded as "The Babe Ruth of Colleges" because of his stellar performance on the mound and at the plate as Columbia's star player. Some expected Babe to give the nineteen-year-old upstart the cold shoulder and perhaps gloat when Gehrig, mostly riding the bench, was finally given a chance to pinch-hit and struck out—many times. Instead, perhaps remembering his own mid-season start with the Sox and the rough time teammates had given him, Babe took Gehrig under his wing. Though different as chalk and cheese, or perhaps because of it, the two developed a strong kinship. "I felt like a father to him," Babe recalled later. And as numbers three and four in the Yankees' batting lineup, they made a formidable team—the *Bambino* and the *Slambino*!

"[Babe is] a pretty big shadow. It gives me lots of room to spread myself."
—Lou Gehrig

If Babe had wished for a do-over year, 1925 would have been it. He showed up at the Yankees' spring training camp in St. Petersburg overweight, out of shape, and looking so rough, Miller Huggins remarked on it. Everyone chalked it up to his wild lifestyle, with good reason. Never one to stay still for long, not even to sleep (certainly not to pass up a good time), and essentially a bachelor because Helen and Dorothy were living at Home Plate Farm full time, Babe took advantage of all the liberties superstardom offered.

> "Babe Ruth ate too much, he played too much and he hit too much.
> What better decade to spawn a hero rooted in overconsumption than the 1920s."
> —"Reflecting the Times," *The Babe Ruth Times*

Babe's usual pre-season shape up at Hot Springs, Arkansas—a routine that had countered his off-season excesses in previous years—didn't work the same magic at thirty. In addition, Babe was battling some intestinal bug and losing. By the time spring training was over and the Yankees boarded the train to begin a series of daily exhibition games on the way back to New York, Babe was really suffering. When they reached Chattanooga, Babe was racked with fever and chills and was too ill for batting practice. But come game time, he rallied as only he could, by rewarding the crowd with two home runs. The next day, in Knoxville, his illness had worsened, but it didn't stop him from hitting another homer.

Finally, whatever kryptonite had infected him, laid Babe flat. After Babe fainted in Asheville, Huggins sent him home. On the train ride back to New York, he fainted twice more, once bashing his head on the sink so hard he knocked himself out. Babe was taken to the hospital and was later operated on for an intestinal abscess. In total, he was in the hospital for almost seven weeks.

On June 1, after missing the first two months of the season, Babe was back on the field. But the "Bellyache Heard Around the World" had infected more than just his belly. He was childish, petulant, and, to put it mildly, argumentative. He and Huggins often butted heads, loudly and publicly. Normally, regardless of how he acted, the Babe respected Huggins and, as his performance showed, responded well to his style of management. But not that season.

> "In Ruth, Miller had two tigers by their tails, for Babe would accept a $5,000 fine and a long suspension with a grin."
> —Sportswriter Grantland Rice, *The Tumult and the Shouting*, 1954

He was fined, suspended, evicted from games, and removed as team captain, but nothing changed his attitude. The trouble wasn't just with Babe, either. The team as a whole performed poorly. It was as though his illness sickened the entire organization. The 1925 Yankees, whom Miller Huggins had called "the best yet" prior to the start of the season, finished seventh in the league. And Babe ended up with only twenty-five homers, his lowest season total between 1919 and 1933.

"The Babe Ruth legend will grow because no other player ever will be able to dim the luster of it."
— Bill Jenkinson, author of *The Year Babe Ruth Hit 104*

"Boomerang" should be added to the Babe's list of nicknames, for just as he had following the 1922 season, Babe bounced back. Taking his abysmal 1925 season as the universe's warning to "shape up or ship out," Babe hired a personal trainer. Artie McGovern, a former boxer, who was one of the earliest fitness gurus in New York, if not the first. He prescribed a strict regime of diet, rest, and exercise, which Babe (the first professional athlete to hire a trainer) fully embraced.

By the start of the 1926 season, Babe was in top form and proved it. He played in 152 of the Yankees' 154 regular season games, hit .372, and helped the Yankees bring home the first of three consecutive American League pennants.

"Every owner of the 16 big-league clubs is united with his manager in the prayer that somehow, somewhere, he can dig up a player who can remotely parallel Babe Ruth."
—F.C. Lane, editor of *Baseball Magazine*

"BASEBALL WAS, IS AND ALWAYS
WILL BE TO ME THE BEST GAME
IN THE WORLD."

"Babe Bows Out," the Pulitzer Prize–winning photo by Nat Fein published in the *New York Herald Tribune*, June 14, 1948. Babe Ruth wore his No. 3 Yankees uniform one last time to commemorate the twenty-fifth anniversary of Yankee Stadium. Babe Ruth retired as the career record-holder in home runs, RBI, total bases, walks, strikeouts, on-base percentage, and slugging percentage, as well as being the single-season record-holder in home runs, total bases, walks, and slugging.

"THE PERSON DOESN'T LIVE WHO WAS BORN WITH EVERYTHING."

"When Ruth signed his 1934 contract he did so with a flourish that indicated he had plenty of practice signing his name."
— *The New York World-Telegram*

Babe Ruth signing baseballs to be awarded to members of the Babe Ruth Boys Club, New York City, 1934. The Babe signed thousands of baseballs and always—surprisingly for a southpaw pitcher—with his right hand. On one barnstorming tour stop in Los Angeles, Babe batted one thousand autographed baseballs off a grandstand roof to a crowd of about ten thousand kids.

"A PART OF CONTROL IS LEARNING TO CORRECT YOUR OWN WEAKNESSES."

"Cobb represents the mauve decades in baseball. Ruth represents the hot cha-cha, and hey nonny, nonny period."
—*The Sporting News*

Babe with Ty Cobb in 1920. With a career batting average of .366, Ty Cobb, the "Georgia Peach," was the superstar—until 1919 when "that big baboon" as he called Babe Ruth, hit the scene. Thus began a fierce rivalry on and off the field. "Later in life, their shared love of golf allowed their original hostility as 'enemies on the ballfield,' to be replaced with a true friendship and admiration for each other's talents." —*BabeRuthCentral.com*

"IT RAINED THAT DAY. EVEN THE HEAVENS WEPT AT THE PASSING OF BABE RUTH."

— ARTHUR DALEY

George Herman "Babe" Ruth died shortly after 8 p.m. on August 16, 1948. He laid in state at the entrance to Yankee Stadium on August 17 and 18. For those two days, the stadium remained open until midnight as an estimated one-hundred thousand people waited in lines for hours to pay their respects.

A Requiem Mass and Funeral were held at St. Patrick's Cathedral in New York City on August 19, 1948. "A crowd ten deep lined both sides of Fifth Avenue" as the funeral procession passed. Connie Mack, owner and manager of the Philadelphia Athletics; sportswriter Fred Lieb; and Babe's former team-mates Whitey Witt, Joe Dugan, and Waite Hoyt served as honorary pallbearers. George Herman Ruth is buried in the Gate of Heaven Cemetery, Hawthorne, New York.

Mourners outside Yankee Stadium waiting to pay their respects to Babe Ruth.

WESTERN UNION

WU A175 DL PD=WUX NEWYORK NY APR 18 418P=

=MRS GEORGE HERMAN RUTH=YANKEE STADIUM=

=MAY I SAY THAT ALL BASEBALL SHARES IN THE PRIDE THAT MUST BE
YOURS TO-DAY. THE "BABE" IS THE SYMBOL OF ALL THINGS WE WOULD
LIKE BASEBALL TO BE AND REPRESENT. HIS CAREER, FABULOUS IN
ITS SUCCESS, IS FIRST OF ALL A STORY OF OPPORTUNITY MADE AND
REALIZED IN THE FINEST AMERICAN TRADITION. BUT IT IS IN HIS
INFLUENCE UPON THE YOUTH OF THE COUNTRY THAT HE HAS MADE HIS
GREATEST AND MOST LASTING CONTRIBUTTIONS TO THE GAME. TO THEM
AND TO ALL OF US HE WILL BE A CONTINUING INSPIRATION. SINCERELY

HORACE C STONEHAM=449P=

WESTERN UNION

WU C031 PD=WUX BOSTON MASS APR 19 1104A=MRS GEORGE H RUTH=

THE ENTIRE PERSONNEL OF THE BOSTON BRAVES FAMILY JOINS BASEBALL
PEOPLE EVERYWHERE IN PAYING TRIBUTE TO THE MEMORY OF YOUR
HUSBAND WHOSE CONTRIBUTIONS TO OUR NATIONAL GAME WILL LIVE LONG
AFTER ALL OF US HAVE SEEN OUR FINAL CONTEST. ON THIS DAY
DEDICATED TO THE BABE, IT IS OUR PRAYER THAT THE YOUNGSTERS
OF TODAY AND TOMORROW MAY ALWAYS LOOK UPON HIM AS ONE WHOSE
SUCCESS IN HIS LIFE'S WORK MUST BY ALL ODDS BE CONSIDERED ONE
OF THE GREAT TRIBUTES TO THE PRIVILEGE OF LIVING IN A DEMOCRACY=

LOUIS R PERINI PRESIDENT BOSTON BRAVES= 1131A..

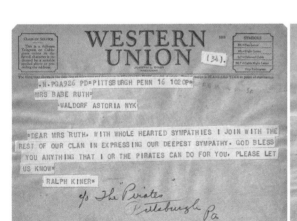

WESTERN UNION

N.PGA926 PD=PITTSBURGH PENN 16 102OP=

MRS BABE RUTH=

WALDORF ASTORIA NYK

=DEAR MRS RUTH. WITH WHOLE HEARTED SYMPATHIES I JOIN WITH THE
REST OF OUR CLAN IN EXPRESSING OUR DEEPEST SYMPATHY. GOD BLESS
YOU ANYTHING THAT I OR THE PIRATES CAN DO FOR YOU. PLEASE LET
US KNOW=

RALPH KINER=

c/o The Pirates
Pittsburgh Pa

WESTERN UNION

NA099 DL PD=WUX BROOKLYN NY 15 250P=

MRS GEORGE H RUTH=

YANKEE STADIUM=

IT IS INDEED APPROPRIATE THAT BASEBALL SHOULD PAY LASTING
HOMAGE TO GEORGE HERMAN RUTH - ONE OF ITS TRULY GREAT
HEROES- ON THE SITE OF HIS MOST MEMORABLE PERFORMANCES.
IT MUST GIVE YOU MUCH SATISFACTION AND COMFORT TO KNOW THAT
HIS SPIRIT LIVES ON IN THE HEARTS AND MINDS OF SPORTS-LOVING
AMERICANS OF ALL AGES AS A CONTINUING INSPIRATION TO YOUTH
AND A FOND MEMORY TO THOSE OF AN EARLIER GENERATION=

BRANCH RICKEY, PRESIDENT   BROOKLYN BASEBALL CLUB=

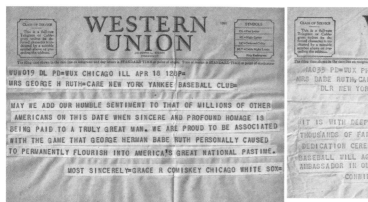

WESTERN UNION

WUW019 DL PD=WUX CHICAGO ILL APR 18 128P=
MRS GEORGE H RUTH=CARE NEW YORK YANKEE BASEBALL CLUB=

MAY WE ADD OUR HUMBLE SENTIMENT TO THAT OF MILLIONS OF OTHER
AMERICANS ON THIS DATE WHEN SINCERE AND PROFOUND HOMAGE IS
BEING PAID TO A TRULY GREAT MAN. WE ARE PROUD TO BE ASSOCIATED
WITH THE GAME THAT GEORGE HERMAN BABE RUTH PERSONALLY CAUSED
TO PERMANENTLY FLOURISH INTO AMERICA'S GREAT NATIONAL PASTIME.

MOST SINCERELY=GRACE R COMISKEY CHICAGO WHITE SOX=

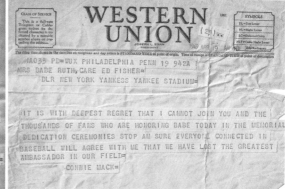

WESTERN UNION

4A035 PD=WUX PHILADELPHIA PENN 19 942A
MRS BABE RUTH, CARE ED FISHER=
DLR NEW YORK YANKESS YANKEE STADIUM=

IT IS WITH DEEPEST REGRET THAT I CANNOT JOIN YOU AND THE
THOUSANDS OF FANS WHO ARE HONORING BABE TODAY IN THE MEMORIAL
DEDICATION CEREMONIES STOP AM SURE EVERYONE CONNECTED IN
BASEBALL WILL AGREE WITH ME THAT WE HAVE LOST THE GREATEST
AMBASSADOR IN OUR FIELD=
CONNIE MACK=

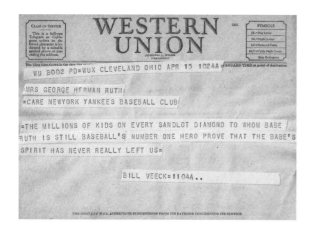

WESTERN UNION

WU B002 PD=WUX CLEVELAND OHIO APR 15 1024A=
MRS GEORGE HERMAN RUTH
=CARE NEWYORK YANKEES BASEBALL CLUB

=THE MILLIONS OF KIDS ON EVERY SANDLOT DIAMOND TO WHOM BABE
RUTH IS STILL BASEBALL'S NUMBER ONE HERO PROVE THAT THE BABE'S
SPIRIT HAS NEVER REALLY LEFT US=

BILL VEECK=1104A..

"It wasn't the baseball records that he left us. It was his legacy of hope."
—Bill Jenkinson, Anniversary Mass at St. Patrick's Cathedral, New York, August 16, 2008

A small selection of telegrams Babe's wife Claire and family received from baseball teams, dignitaries, and friends the world over at the time of his death.

"THE ONE THING A GOOD CATCHER MUST HAVE IS NERVE."

"What I am, what I have, what I am going to leave behind me—all this I owe to the game of baseball, without which I would have come out of St. Mary's Industrial School in Baltimore as a tailor, and a pretty bad one, at that.
—Babe Ruth

St. Mary's "Red Sox" team photo, 1912. Catcher "Jidge" is in the top row, left. The Red Sox, a team of St. Mary's best players, traveled throughout Baltimore playing against company and college teams—and as the banner shows, winning!

"BASE STEALING ISN'T SO MUCH A MATTER OF SPEED AS IT IS A QUESTION OF CATCHING THE OPPONENTS OFF GUARD, GETTING A GOOD LEAD, AND THEN BEING ABLE TO START FAST."

"They all look at him, and they call him 'fat'??? . . . He stole home!"
- John Kennelly, *Bube Ruth: The Life Behind the Legend* film documentary, 1998

Production still of "Babe Dugan" sliding into base from the 1927 movie *Babe Comes Home*. Babe stealing bases wasn't just the stuff of movies; in his MLB career, Babe Ruth stole 123 bases, including stealing home ten times!

"LOVE THE GAME OF BASEBALL AND BASEBALL WILL LOVE YOU."

During the 1926 World Series against the St. Louis Cardinals, upon learning a boy named Johnny Sylvester was in bad shape after being kicked in the head by a horse, both teams sent him a package that included two baseballs, one signed by Cardinal players and one signed by five Yankees players. On the ball signed by the Yankees, Babe Ruth wrote "I'll knock a homer for you." Did he do it? Even better! The Colossus of Clout hit three home runs in the fourth game, four total for the series. After the series, Babe visited Johnny, who told him he was sorry the Yanks lost.

Babe with Johnny Sylvester at Yankee Stadium. Through the years Babe kept in touch with Johnny via letters like this one from December 16, 1926. When the Babe was seriously ill, Johnny repaid the kindness by visiting him.

"*Babe*" *Ruth's coming to Town!*

AFTER BREAKING TEN (10) RECORDS IN THE WORLDS SERIES

Pantages Theatre   -   Portland

17/12/26.

Dear Johnny

They tell me you are once more up and around ready for the spring training season. Here's hoping that you will have a very merry Christmas and that the New Year will bring you a full measure of health and happiness.

You and I have a lot to remember about the 1926 World Series and when the Yanks win the Championship next year I hope that you will be with me in person at the Stadium to help win another pennant.

Sincerely
"Babe" Ruth

Babe Ruth in action during a game at Fenway Park.

"THERE ISN'T A MAN IN BASEBALL TODAY WHO ISN'T HAPPIER WHEN HE'S UP THERE AT THE PLATE WITH A STICK IN HIS HAND."

"All I can say is that the balls Ruth hit out of the park got smaller quicker than anybody else's."
—Walter Johnson

"If the Babe had played in the current baseball climate with the leagues expanded to twenty-six teams and the talent watered down, there's no telling how many home runs he would have hit."
—Hank Greenberg, *The Story of My Life*, 1989

"EVERY STRIKE BRINGS ME CLOSER TO THE NEXT HOME RUN."

"He was better than me. He was the best that ever lived. That big joker hit it clear out of the park."
—Guy Bush

Babe Ruth with Braves teammates centerfielder Wally Berger and leftfielder Hal Lee. On May 26, 1935, in a game against the Pittsburg Pirates, Babe went four-for-four, hitting three home runs—his 712th, 713th, and 714th, which set an MLB career home run record that stood until 1974—and driving in six runs. Number 714 was truly a "moonshot." It stands as the first-ever hit over the right field grandstand at Forbes Field. The hit was measured to have flown 524 feet. Pirates Pitcher Guy Bush later recalled, "It was the longest cockeyed ball I ever saw hit in my life."

BUNYAN BABE

"The Babe had that wink—he'd wink at fans in the stands, people on the street, at the opposing pitcher, at fielders on the opposition as he circled the bases trotting out a home run. The winking Babe said: 'This is easy. This is a lot of fun.'"
—Harvey Frommer

Babe Ruth wasn't the first person to have his signature carved into a Louisville Slugger, but Babe's is the signature most folks remember. Why? Because Babe Ruth, the Great Bambino, is the player everyone—baseball fans and otherwise—know. That all caps with sparkles still-the-most-recognizable-baseball-player of all time BABE a la product endorsements, speaking engagements, barnstorming tours, and publicity stunts—including, in July of 1926, catching a baseball dropped from an airplane three hundred feet overhead doing eighty miles per hour—that "Babe the Brand" BABE was partly the doing of Babe's agent/manager, Christy Walsh. But only partly.

One thing no one, anywhere, ever called Babe Ruth was shy. He was a talker who could, would, and did talk to anyone. A confident, articulate, sound bite factory, Babe was a favorite with newswriters and radio broadcasters too. He had a quick wit, easy laugh, and clear, distinctive voice in a time when radio, in its fledgling days of crackly microphones and spotty reception, needed strong recognizable voices. By the time the first major league baseball game was broadcast on August 5, 1921, and the first World Series in 1923, Babe's voice was familiar to American listeners—more so than the president's. Warren Harding was the first president to have his voice transmitted over the radio, but that wasn't until June 14, 1922.

"... with Walsh's help, Ruth would become the first ballplayer
to be paid as much for what he did off the field as for what he did on it."
—Jane Leavy, *The Big Fella*

From the moment Jacob Ruppert threw in with "Cap" Huston to buy the Yankees in 1915, he had one goal and one goal only: to own a winning team. Ed Barrow and Miller Huggins shared that goal and set out to make it happen. Acquiring Babe Ruth from the

Red Sox was one of their first steps toward realizing that goal.

> "Ruth was the only ball player I have known who could turn out
> capacity crowds every time. He did this in every city the Yankees played."
> —Sportswriter Grantland Rice, *The Tumult and the Shouting*

"BABE" was the headline in the newspaper Americans read over coffee. His face grinning out at them from the cereal boxes and bread wrappers on their tables. His was the name on the skivvies beneath their britches. And, with a few movie credits under his belt, he was their matinee idol. Starstruck, everyone flocked to his games, any game, anywhere, anytime the Bambino was playing, some to watch baseball, many to watch him. Babe was *the* fan magnet. He made baseball fans of non-fans. His fame paved the road for the Yankees' future success. More fans meant more money at the ticket booth. More money to buy more talent. And, come contract renewal time, money to keep Babe happy—within reason.

> "Carrying his 221 pounds jauntily and proclaiming a no-compromise program on his $100,000 salary demand, Babe
> Ruth came to New York today for an anticipated battle with Col. Jake Ruppert, Yankee owner, over a 1927 contract."
> —*Leominster Daily Enterprise*, March 2, 1927

In 1927, after an extended push-pull, Ruppert locked Babe in with a three-year contract at an annual salary of $70,000. At the time, no other Yankees' player made anywhere near that much. In his book *Babe: The Legend Comes to Life*, Robert W. Creamer verified the Yankees' 1927 salaries:

> "After Ruth, at $70,000, the next highest paid player was Pennock, at $17,500. Muesel made $13,000,
> Dugan and Hoyt $12,000, Combs $10,000. Gehrig made $8,000. Lazzeri $8,000."

The Yankees 1927 squad was pure talent. Offensively, the pitching squad (Waite Hoyt, Herb Pennock, Urban Shocker, Dutch Reuther, and even the rookie pitcher Wilcy Moore) was a force. Coupled with the batting lineup (Earle Combs, Mark Koenig, Babe Ruth, Lou Gehrig, Bob Meusel, and Tony Lazzeri—called Murderers' Row by opposing pitchers), the team became legendary.

"Those fellows not only beat you but they tear your heart out. I wish the season was over."
—Senators' first baseman Joe Judge, after the Yanks crushed Washington 21–1

Beginning with an 8–3 Opening Day win, the Yankees were in first place or tied for first the entire 1927 season. **Win-Win-Win.** Combs hitting, Koenig hitting, Ruth hitting, Gehrig hitting, Meusel hitting, Lazzeri hitting, game after game . . . all that winning might have become tedious if, during the June 23 match against Boston, the quiet, unassuming twenty-four-year-old Lou Gehrig—usually Babe's shadow—hadn't belted out one, two, three home runs in one game.

No big-league player had ever knocked out three home runs in one game at Fenway Park before! Babe, the Behemoth of Bash, had yet to hit three homers in one game! That's when everyone started counting. On June 29, Gehrig hit his twenty-fourth home run of the season to tie Babe Ruth. Unheard of! Babe had never had anyone—let alone a teammate—rattle his throne. "The Great American Home Run Derby" was on!

June 30: Gehrig and Ruth both hit number twenty-six.
July 2: Gehrig pulled ahead.

"There will never be another guy like the Babe. I get more kick out of seeing him hit one than I do from hitting one myself."
—Gehrig to Ford C. Frick, *New York Evening Journal*, July 2, 1927

July 3: Ruth struck back with the longest homer ever hit in Griffith Stadium. The count was tied at twenty-seven.
On July 5: Gehrig led twenty-eight to twenty-five.

"The Odds Favor Gehrig to Beat Out Ruth in Home Run Derby."
—*New York Telegram*, July 5, 1927

Hillerich and Bradley, makers of Louisville Slugger bats sporting both Gehrig and Ruth's signatures, shipped Home Run Derby scorecard posters to all their suppliers. School kids, baseball buffs, and everyone in between were tallying homers.

"There has never been anything like it . . . Even as these lines are batted out on the office typewriter, youths dash out of the AP and UP ticker room every two or three minutes shouting, 'Ruth hit one! Gehrig just hit another one!'"
—Paul Gallico, *New York Daily News*

At the time of the home run race, off the field, Ruth and Gehrig were pals. On the field they were teammates, and at the plate, friendly rivals.

"Any rivalry between them [Ruth and Gehrig] for the title appeared at worst good-natured competition."
—Ford C. Frick, *New York Evening Journal*, July 2, 1927

By the end of July, Gehrig was one up on Ruth, thirty-five to thirty-four.

"[Gehrig is] one of the finest fellows in the game."
—Babe Ruth to Richards Vidmer, *The New York Times*, August 1, 1927

Throughout July and August, The Big Bam and The Iron Horse were never more than two home runs apart. Folks all over the country were keeping close watch. On game days, newspapers increased the number of editions they printed from one or two per day, to putting out a new edition with an updated tally almost every time Gehrig or Ruth batted.

By the end of August, Ruth was two up, forty-three to forty-one.

September 2, Lou smacked out two homers; Babe hit one to keep the lead, forty-four to forty-three.

By September 6, they were tied again at forty-four.

"Like two mighty boxers they slugged home runs trying to out-do each other and everyone else in 1927."
—Harvey Frommer

Then Gehrig hit a slump. Maybe the pressure got to be too much, or worry might have messed up his game. His mother, with whom he was extremely close, was ill in the hospital. Whatever the cause, Gehrig went nineteen games without a hit. The Derby was finished, but Babe was not.

Every season since 1921, when Babe had slammed out fifty-nine homers to best his own single-season home run record again, reporters had been asking him if this would be the year he'd hit sixty. At the start of the 1927 season, just as he'd done every other year, Babe assured them he was sure going to try. In 1927, reporters scoffed. They didn't think after twelve seasons of hard playing and hard living, Babe had a sixty-home run season in him.

They were wrong.

On September 29, in a home game against the Washington Senators, Babe homered twice to match his 1921 record of fifty-nine (which was more than any other team's total). That caught their attention.

September 30 was the second-to-last game of the regular season. In the bottom of the eighth with the score tied 2–2, Babe set aside his warm-up bats. He took a swipe at Senators' pitcher Tom Zachary's first pitch for a strike. Then Zachary sent a fastball whizzing. What happened next is truly the stuff of fiction. As described in *ESPN*'s real-time historical retelling "1927: The Diary of Myles Thomas":

"The crack of Ruth's bat sets off an explosion that lights up the Stadium, like a bolt of lightning. All of us—the fans in the stands and the players on both teams—rise as one, pulled out of our seats by the flight of the ball. Ruth slowly leaves the batter's box, taking his time to admire his handiwork. He lets his bat fall from his hands, as he has hundreds of times before—more than any man who has ever walked the earth—and slowly strides up the first base line . . . It's not simply Ruth's 60th home run. It's immortality."

Babe's record of sixty homers in one season stood for thirty-four years, until Roger Maris topped it in 1961. (For the record, Maris's season was ten games and fifty at-bats longer.) Together, King Babe and the Crowned Prince of Crash, Lou Gehrig, tallied more than one hundred home runs in 1927, with 338 RBI and 307 runs. In an almost anticlimactic ending, the Yankees finished nineteen games ahead of the Athletics with a record-setting 110–44–1 to set what is still the American League all-time highest single-season winning percentage (.721). Which, they capped at the 1927 Fall Classic by besting the Pittsburg Pirates 4–0 to take home another World Series title.

"It is our desire to have a pennant winner each year indefinitely. New York fans want championship ball, and the Yankees can be counted on to provide it."
—Miller Huggins, *The Sporting News*, August 4, 1927

When the series ended, Babe and Gehrig took their show on the road. Christy Walsh, who managed both players, cobbled together a roster of players and had jerseys made up: "The Bustin' Babes" and "The Larrupin' Lous."

Because there were no major league teams west or south of St. Louis—and wouldn't be until 1958—for fans and players, these postseason barnstorming tours were a win-win. In the days before television, they gave fans in other parts of the country a chance to watch big-league players in action. Plus, they were a chance for players to make extra money. In those days, Babe aside, even the best professional players didn't earn much during the season, so they needed it. On that 1927 tour, which included twenty-one stops from Rhode Island to San Diego, Babe earned a salary plus a percentage of ticket sales; Gehrig pocketed more than he had for the whole regular season.

During the barnstorming tour—which would have been more aptly named baseball's "Goodwill Tour"—arrangements were made for the big-league players to play with and against Negro Leagues teams, company and college teams, and home-town heroes. Babe and half of the big-league players on the tour would become the Bustin' Babes, while Gehrig and the rest would become the Larrupin' Lous.

The games were pure chaos, with kids running onto the field and grabbing balls and people stealing bases, pestering players for autographs, and snapping photos. As often as not, games were called because they ran out of baseballs. Along the way, Babe—baseball's unofficial Goodwill Ambassador—made sure fans got what they wanted: hits! Lots and lots of hits and a whopper of a good time.

"Ruth is a big, likeable kid. He has been well named, Babe. Ruth will never grow up and probably never will."
—Billy Evans, umpire

In 1928, Ruth and Gehrig treated fans to another derby, this one for RBI—Gehrig won 147–146. Both players' regular season was lackluster in comparison to the previous year. Babe suffered from one ailment after another and "only" managed fifty-four home runs. (Those fifty-four were still twenty-three more than any other player in the MLB hit that year.) But come the Fall Classic, the dangerous duo made up for it by putting on a stellar show. The Babe batted .625 with ten hits in four games, three of them homers; Gehrig batted .545 with four home runs and nine RBI. And with a little help from the rest of the batting lineup, they bested the Cardinals in four games.

"The able Ruth, heralded as a cripple, pounded the crack St. Louis hurlers as if they were but Class 'C' pitchers in a bad slump."
—The Ottawa Citizen, October 12, 1928

The Babe was living large, still basking in the afterglow of the Yankees second-in-a-row Championship when life interrupted. On January 11, 1929, his estranged wife Helen died in a housefire. Headlines went from "Star Babe" to "Scandalous Babe" in one news cycle as rumors about the cause of the fire circulated.

"Let Tragedy Drop, Babe Ruth Begs as Police Investigate Murder Hints."
—*Albany Evening News*, January 15, 1929

Frankly speaking, "family" had been an afterthought for Babe since 1925, when he and Helen had officially separated. At the time of her death, Helen was living with someone; Babe was head-over-heels for his future wife, Claire Hodgson; and, although only seven, Dorothy was at boarding school. Aside from off-season visits and holidays, Babe rarely saw her. Suddenly, tragically, their bubble burst. Along with fending off the usual crush of reporters, Babe was fielding questions about Helen's death and worrying about how to protect a daughter he barely knew.

On April 17, 1929, George Herman Ruth and Claire Hodgson were married at St. Gregory's Church on West 90th Street in Manhattan. To avoid drawing a crowd, they sneaked off to the church pre-dawn for a 5:45 a.m. ceremony. Even with all the secrecy, hundreds of fans cheered when the couple emerged from the church. In response to shouted questions about where the couple were going on their honeymoon, Babe shouted back, "The ballpark!"

"Babe Ruth and Former Ziegfeld Follies Star Married Early Today"

"It was the start of a busy day in the busy life of baseball's best-paid employee, for at the Yankee Stadium this afternoon he expected to shoulder his bat and begin earning the yearly salary of $70,000 with which he hopes to furnish an apartment and buy groceries for his bride."
—*United Press*, April 17, 1929

As it turns out, the season opener, originally scheduled for April 16, was postponed again, so it wasn't played until the following afternoon. On April 18, with his new bride watching in the stands, Babe celebrated their nuptials as only Babe could: by hitting a home run. As he circled the bases, Babe blew Claire a kiss.

After the wedding, Babe and Dorothy moved in with Claire and her daughter,

Julia, to their apartment at 345 West 88th Street in Manhattan. Claire's mother, Carrie, and two brothers, Eugene and Hubert, moved in as well. The following October, the couple adopted each other's daughters. For the first time in his life, Babe was living a "normal homelife." Even with all he had, those two words—"normal" and "homelife"—had never been linked. Prior to that, the closest Babe had come to having a homelife were those first months of his marriage to Helen, when the couple lived in Baltimore near his family and had getaways to Home Plate Farm. But those times weren't real life, they were off season. By all accounts, having a "normal homelife" with Claire and their family was good for Babe.

> "Daddy and Mother loved entertaining people at their home. Daddy loved his home and all the things that went on—all the holidays. They would almost always have a New Year's party and I can remember some of the various people that used to come—Hoagy Carmichael would come and play the piano. That was just fabulous."
> —Julia Ruth Stevens

The honeymoon season ended abruptly when Yankees manager Miller Huggins died unexpectedly on September 25. His death, after almost twelve seasons, and the succession of managers that followed (Art Fletcher, Bob Shawkey, and finally, in 1931, Joe McCarthy) affected the whole team. But for Babe, each change of manager rankled him, and—after former teammate Shawkey didn't work out—he set his sights on moving from player to management.

By 1930, the Great Depression had hit America hard and heavy. There was joblessness, homelessness, bread lines on the east and west coasts, drought, and the Dust Bowl in Middle America. That January, when contract time came around, Babe asked for a raise to $85,000 per year. The Bambino was no baby anymore. The year 1930 marked sixteen years since he'd left St. Mary's to join Jack Dunn's Baltimore Orioles. In baseball time, he was an oldster. Even by today's standards, with all the advancements in training, commitment, and fitness, the longest MLB playtime a rookie can expect is five or six seasons. Sixteen seasons playing pro ball had taken its toll. After years of chasing down balls while hauling around that mighty barrel-shaped torso, his signature matchstick legs were giving him problems. Babe was also suffering from headaches and was beset by other injuries. After a few tense months of haggling, he and owner, Jacob Ruppert, settled on a two-year, $80,000 per year contract. Value-wise, it was a great deal for the Yankees.

"He was also getting more money than anyone else in baseball, and more than twice as much as anybody on the Yankees. But he was worth every penny of it . . . He brought in two dollars through the turnstiles for every dollar Ruppert paid him."
—Eleanor Gehrig, Lou Gehrig's wife, *DiMaggio: The Last American Knight* by Joseph Durso

Babe was the best show around. He was tops in the American League with forty-nine home runs, tops in walks, and still tops with fans. Regardless of where the Yankees were playing, fans managed to scrape together enough coins to come to games. And why wouldn't they? In grim times, one thing they could count on was The Big Bam.

"Don't tell me about Ruth. I've seen what he did to people; fans driving miles in open wagons through the prairies of Oklahoma to see him in exhibition games as we headed north in the spring. Kids, men, women, worshippers all, hoping to get his name on a torn, dirty piece of paper, or hoping for a grunt of recognition when they said 'Hi Ya, Babe.' He never let them down, not once. He was the greatest crowd pleaser of them all."
—Waite Hoyt, "Shortstops: Waite Hoyt Remember the Babe" by Larry Brunt, *baseballhall.org*

On April 30, 1933, Babe blasted a homer in the second game of a doubleheader against the Red Sox. As he walked off the field, he had no clue that the longest home run slump of his career was about to begin.

The Babe was thirty-eight, early in his twentieth season playing pro ball. He'd maintained his winter workout regime with Artie McGovern, hunted, fished, and golfed plenty prior to spring training and, despite reporter Edward J. Neil snarking how "he still looks as if he'd stuffed a watermelon under his shirt," announced that he was "feeling better than he had in five years." A home run slump was not in his plans.

For ordinary players, the Babe's performance in the weeks following the April 30 game would have been fine, good even. He got some hits, RBI, scored runs—his batting average hovered around .300. But the King of Clout was no ordinary player. "Fine" was not fine.

Leigh Montville noted in **The Big Bam: The Life and Times of Babe Ruth** that on May 23, Babe told Joe McCarthy, "I feel good. I think I'm going to bust one today." And bust one he did—it sailed right into "Ruthville" (the nickname for Yankee Stadium's right-field bleachers because his hits landed there so often). The longest home run slump of his career had lasted less than a month. Other MLB players go years without hitting a home run.

On October 1, 1933, Babe pitched one last game as a Yankee, against his former team the Red Sox. At thirty-eight, he was overweight and plagued with injuries. It was the last game of the season. His appearance on the mound was mostly to boost attendance, and maybe to prove he still had it. Although his pitching was a far cry from what it had been in his early years, he lasted all nine innings, only surrendered twelve hits and five runs, walked three with no strikeouts, and chalked up one final win. The game ended Yankees 6, Sox 5.

After the game, someone asked Babe if he'd ever get back on the mound, to which he gave an emphatic, "Never again!"

> "I had such a sore arm, I had to eat with my right hand for a week!"
> —Babe Ruth after the October 1, 1933, game

By all accounts, pulling off a win like that after not having pitched in over three years was, what reporters called, a "Ruthian" feat. To top it off, in the fifth inning, the Babe thumbed his nose at naysayers by knocking out his thirty-fourth home run of the season, giving him two more than Lou Gehrig to finish tops among all Yankee batters and placing him second in the league to Philadelphia's Jimmie Foxx. Be that as it may, thirty-four homers was not forty-eight, not "Ruthian" enough for the guy who invented the term.

Prior to the start of the 1933 season, Babe announced to the world that he had three ambitions for his baseball career: the first to play in ten World Series, which he'd done; the second was to complete twenty years of baseball, which he'd do that season; the third and final goal: "I hope to boost my home run total to seven hundred. I hope to do that by hitting at least forty-eight this year."

On July 13, 1934, at Detroit's Navin Field—a lucky Friday the 13th for the Yankees—Babe launched one of Tommy Bridges's pitches over the right field fence onto Plum Street—over five hundred feet. It was the Babe's fourteenth homer of the season and the seven hundredth of his career. (At that point, only two other players had passed the three hundred career homer mark: Lou Gehrig with 314 and Rogers Hornsby with 301.) With number seven hundred in the record book, Babe checked DONE on the third and last goal on his list. Four days later, he drew his two-thousandth career walk.

"He [Babe] had six of the most extraordinary seasons, from 1926–1932, that any ballplayer's ever had. He averaged over 50 home runs a year for six years."
—Robert W. Creamer

"A LITTLE FELLA IS AS GOOD AS ANYBODY IF HE KNOWS HIS STUFF."

In 1947, Babe became National Director of the American Legion Junior Baseball, which was sponsored by Ford Motor Company. The Legion funded local teams and hosted baseball tournaments. As Director, Babe toured the country, attending games, giving players tips, and signing autographs.

Babe checking out a young player's throwing arm, New York, 1939.

June 12, 1939, National Baseball Hall of Fame, Cooperstown, New York. Front row (left to right): Eddie "Cocky" Collins, Babe Ruth, Connie Mack, Cy Young; back row (left to right): Honus "The Flying Dutchman" Wagner, Grover Cleveland "Old Pete" Alexander, Tris "The Grey Eagle" Speaker, Napoleon "The Frenchman" Lajoie, "Gorgeous George" Sisler, and "The Big Train" Walter Johnson. Ty Cobb is not pictured.

"HEROES GET REMEMBERED, BUT LEGENDS NEVER DIE."

In 1936, the first class was voted into the National Baseball Hall of Fame. It included Ty Cobb, Walter Johnson, Christy Mathewson, Honus Wagner, and Babe Ruth. Candidates were nominated and voted on by members of the members of the Baseball Writers' Association of America. During that first election, only "modern-era" ballplayers (i.e., players whose professional careers began after 1900) were considered. A total of 226 ballots were cast and a player needed to receive 170 votes for election. Cobb received 222 votes, Johnson 189, Mathewson 205, and Ruth and Honus Wagner tied with 215 votes. All eleven living inductees from the 1936–39 classes attended the ceremony. Lou Gehrig was also in the class of 1939, but he was elected later in the year.

"I LIKE TO LIVE AS BIG AS I CAN."

"He was a walking, talking highlight film each and every day of his life, both on and off the field."
—Mike Barnicle, *ESPN The Magazine*, September 14, 1999

"R is for Ruth,
To tell you the Truth,
There's no more to be said,
Just R is for Ruth"
—from "Lineup for Yesterday" by Ogden Nash, *Sport* magazine, January 1949

Babe flying high, Sea Spray Beach, Palm Beach Florida, January 30, 1930.

"IF I'D TRIED FOR THEM DINKY SINGLES I COULD'VE BATTED AROUND SIX HUNDRED."

Babe Ruth with President Herbert Hoover at the November 11, 1933, Stanford vs. USC football game. In 1930, Babe signed a two-year contract with the Yankees at a salary of $80,000 per year. After signing, a reporter pointed out that the new salary was $5,000 more than the US president earned and asked if Babe thought he should be paid more than President Hoover.

"Why not?" Babe tossed back. "I had a better year than he did."

"A LITTLE EXERCISE OF THE NOODLE WILL SAVE A LOT OF WEAR AND TEAR ON THE ARM."

"Babe Ruth is part of an elite set of pitchers in Major League history whose career on the mound spanned at least ten seasons and NEVER once included a losing record!"
—BaseballAlmanac.com

"He was fast; he had a good arm; there was nothing about baseball he couldn't do."
—John Kennelly

"I'm prouder of my pitching 29 consecutive World Series scoreless innings than I am of my subsequent home-run records with the Yankees."

— Babe Ruth

Babe Ruth throwing lefty, circa 1921.

"WHAT I AM, WHAT I HAVE, WHAT I AM GOING TO LEAVE BEHIND ME—ALL THIS I OWE TO THE GAME OF BASEBALL."

"It was at St. Mary's that I met and learned to love the greatest man I've ever known. He was the father I needed."
—Babe Ruth in *The Babe Ruth Story*

"I never forget the first time I saw him [Brother Matthias] hit a ball. The baseball in 1902 was a lump of mush, but Brother Matthias would stand at the end of the yard, throw the ball up with his left hand, and give it a terrific belt with the bat he held in his right hand. The ball would carry 350 feet, a tremendous knock in those days. I would watch him bug-eyed."
—Babe Ruth in "The Kids Can't Take It if We Don't Give It," *Guideposts Magazine*, October 1948

Babe standing in front of a car with Brother Matthias at St. Mary's, circa 1925. The car is possibly one of two that Babe bought for Brother Matthias.

1935 BRAVES AND BEYOND

"Babe Ruth, the hero of all our baseball days."
—New York City Mayor William O' Dwyer

Babe kicked off the 1934 season with what was literally a bang-up spring in St. Petersburg. As was his habit, he arrived in St. Petersburg in February, to get in plenty of golf before spring training. "I am depending on golf to help me regain my top-notch physical condition," he told reporters after scoring the Jungle Club's first-ever seventeenth hole double eagle. By all accounts, he enjoyed "probably the greatest spring of his twenty-year career in the majors. "He has cracked out six home runs in seven games, driving in sixteen runs and scored ten," noted Jeff Moshier in the *St. Petersburg Evening Independent*, a sentiment Ruth himself seconded in a *New York Times* article, in which he credited his hitting to "that new ball," saying, "I've been hitting them high and far, like no other ball I've ever swung at." In fact, "that new ball," Babe referred to was not "new." It was the same kind the American League had been using since 1931, newly adopted by the National League.

To drive his point home and beyond, in an exhibition game at Waterfront Park on March 25, against, ironically, the Boston Braves, Babe blasted his legendary "West Coast Inn Home Run" when he, as Pete Norris of the *St. Pete Times* put it, "Socked a [Huck] Betts pitch 10,000 leagues to right field . . ." [The ball] "actually hit the second-floor porch of the West Coast Inn, with the sphere first bouncing (on a fly) on its front walkway, which, at is closest point, was 610-feet from where Babe smashed his phenomenal 'four-bagger'" ("The Legend of Babe Ruth's West Coast Inn Home Run," *BabeRuthCentral.com*).

"It flew far beyond 500 feet, and may have reached the forbidden distance of 600 feet. For many years, I have steadfastly believed that no human being could hit a baseball 600 feet, but, based on new research on this blow, I admit I was probably mistaken."
—Bill Jenkinson, about Babe's March 25, 1934, "West Coast Inn Home Run," *Baseball's Ultimate Power: Ranking the All-Time Great Distance Home Run Hitters*, 2010

Later, a team of longball researchers (which included Tim Reid, Bob Ward, Bill Jenkinson, and Bruce Orser) confirmed the actual distance in air the ball flew was "no less than 610 feet."

"[Babe] demonstrated historically phenomenal power during Spring Season, including hitting what is likely the longest home run ever hit off major league pitching."
—Tim Reid, baseball historian

When Babe returned to St. Petersburg in 1948, locals asked him what his greatest accomplishment there had been.

"The day I hit the . . . ball against that . . . hotel!"
—Babe Ruth in "Babe Ruth's Longest Home Run" by Will Michaels, *northeastjournal.org*

Babe finished spring training with a .429 batting average. From there the rest of the 1934 season was anti-climactic. Statistically speaking, it was a good season. The Yankees placed second in the American League, seven games behind the Tigers. Babe's twenty-two homers and eighty-four RBI (second only to Lou Gehrig) were still almost twice as many as anyone else on the team (Lazzeri racked up fourteen). And, on July 13, he had carved the seven hundredth notch in his career home run tally. Even so, the battleship of a team the Yankees had become while Miller Huggins was manager had still not righted itself. And twenty years of hard playing and hard living had taken a toll on the Babe. As the scoreboards showed, he could still swing and make it count, but his running and fielding had deteriorated. Prior to the season, he himself had said as much.

"Today, at 40,* the Babe admits himself that he is all but through. He hopes to play in 100 games for the Yankees this season but finally agrees with the boys that his days as a player are numbered."
—Jeff Moshier, "Babe Fools Experts by Fast Start," *St. Petersburg Evening Independent* per "Babe Ruth's Longest Home Run" by Will Michaels.
*It was actually Babe's thirty-ninth birthday.

The truth was Yankees' owner Colonel Jacob Ruppert was tired of paying Babe's salary (still the highest in MLB). From where Ruppert was sitting, the Yankees didn't need Babe Ruth anymore. Despite having lost the pennant to the Tigers, they were still the most popular team in the League. Besides, they had the Iron Horse, Lou Gehrig—who'd outplayed Babe to win the 1934 AL Triple Crown—and Dickey, Lazzeri, Crosetti, Saltzgaver, and Selkirk.

Besides Ruppert and everyone else knew Babe wanted to move into a management position. Ever since 1930, when Bob Shawkey had been sent packing after the Yankees finished the season in third, Babe had made his desire to move into management clear.

"I wouldn't be choosy about what club it is. The lower the club, the better for me.
If I improved it and got it up in the race, I would get credit for it."
—Babe Ruth to Leigh Montville, *The Big Bam: The Life and Times of Babe Ruth*

In actuality, Ruppert had no intention of offering Babe a management position with the Yankees (although he did offer him managership of the Newark Bears, a AAA franchise and their next most important team). Nor, apparently, did Ruppert want Babe managing any other Major League team. Despite having publicly stated on October 19, 1933, "I think Ruth will make a splendid manager. He's settled down and is very serious about his future . . . I'd like to keep Ruth with the Yankees, but I'll not interfere if he gets a chance to better himself" (**Associated Press**), when the Cincinnati Reds approached Ruppert about offering Babe the manager position, "All they got was an emphatic 'No!'" (as disclosed by Larry MacPhail, the Reds' general manager, to the **New York Times** on December 30, 1933). A gentleman's agreement between Babe and Detroit Tigers' owner, Frank Navin, similarly evaporated.

"One thing Ruth had, and one thing which would have helped as
a manger had he ever been granted the opportunity, was that he was a grand competitor."
—Tom Meany, *Babe Ruth: The Big Moments and the Big Fella*

The reason why Babe was passed up for a management position in the Majors, despite interest and offers, will remain murky. Many baseball buffs believe it's because Babe would have integrated baseball were he in a position to do so. Throughout his career,

Babe played baseball with and against players from all backgrounds. In his essay "Babe Ruth and the Issue of Race," Bill Jenkinson noted:

> "When the [1920] season ended, Ruth received hundreds of invitations to barnstorm anywhere he wanted to go. Of the approximately fifteen games that Babe selected, five were against so-called Negro League teams. Ruth then sailed to Cuba, where he joined John McGraw's Giants to play nine more contests versus a combination of Latino and Negro ballplayers. Again, the message was clear: if the sport's transcendent figure played without reservation against Black ballplayers, why shouldn't everyone else?"

Graham McNamee once asked Babe who he regarded as the greatest player of all time. "You mean Major Leaguers?" Ruth asked. "No," McNamee said, "the greatest player anywhere." "In that case," Ruth replied, "I'd pick John Henry Lloyd." Future Hall of Famer "Pop" Lloyd was a power-hitting shortstop and manager in the Negro Leagues.

Jenkinson went on to note how off-season Babe chose—because, off season the choice of who to play and where was his—"He [Babe] played games against Negro League teams in 1926, 1927, 1928, 1929, and showed up again in Kansas City in 1931 to compete with the Monarchs. That contest under the lights was rained out, but Ruth was there and ready to go."

At the end of February 1935, shortly before the start of spring training, Ruppert and Boston Braves' owner Judge Emil Fuchs came to an agreement to offer Babe a deal. The Babe would join the Boston Braves, with the title of "Vice President," as a player and assistant manager of the team for a straight salary of $25,000, a share of the profits, stock options, and an opportunity to become part owner. And so, after fifteen seasons with the New York Yankees, which included seven American League Pennants and four World Series wins, the Great Bambino, the Colossus of Clout, the Sultan of Swat traded navy pinstripes for the Boston Braves' red and blue.

"The success of the Yankees is no longer intertwined with, and dependent upon, the success of Ruth."
—Jacob Ruppert, "Ruppert Sees Boom Year and Pennant for Yanks," *New York Telegram*

"Colonel Ruppert sent him a contract for a dollar a year and gave him his unconditional release."
—Julia Ruth Stevens, HBO *Babe Ruth* documentary

On March 5, 1935, Babe played his first game as a Boston Brave, a spring training exhibition game—and blasted a home run! Thinking his long-held dream of transitioning from player to manager was finally coming true, Babe was feeling good about his future with the Braves.

What everyone but Babe seemed to know, however, was that the whole VP-manager-potential owner thing was a bunch of malarky. What Fuchs really wanted was a fan magnet, and Babe was the best around! He started the 1935 season with a bang—literally! During the April 16 opening day game at Braves Field, in front of about twenty thousand cheering fans, Babe nailed his first dinger of the season.

It didn't take long for Babe to realize he'd been duped. The Braves had no intention of letting him manage. Fuchs is "a dirty double-crosser" who "would double cross a hot bun," Babe is quoted as having said in *The Big Bam: The Life and Times of Babe Ruth* by Leigh Montville.

Along with his badly bruised ego came the expected aches and pains of being "fat and forty," including persistent colds and headaches. His legs ached. His eyes were giving him trouble. He couldn't run. And his fielding was so terrible that three of the Braves' pitchers threatened to go on strike if Ruth was in the lineup.

"During the 1935 Braves training season I was a big draw. People were curious to see how I looked in a National League uniform, but the harder I tried the worse I did."
—Babe Ruth in *The Babe Ruth Story*

Before long, the novelty of having Babe on the team wasn't enough to keep the stands full, especially when (more often than not) it meant watching him warm the bench. It wasn't always injuries keeping him from playing. As aware as anyone of how poorly he was playing, Babe benched himself sometimes in hopes of giving the Braves a fighting chance at a win.

"Even Ruth, in his decline was monumental. Players would stop in pre-game workout to watch him struggling in the field . . . They couldn't believe what they were seeing. The great statue beginning to crack and topple . . . The god turning human."
—Bill Mazer, HBO *Baseball* documentary

While the Babe was down, he wasn't out—yet! On May 25, 1935, the Braves faced off against the Pirates in a day game at Forbes Field. Prior to the game, the Pirates' starting pitcher, Red Lucas, asked Waite Hoyt, a former Yankee, the best strategy for pitching to the Babe.

> "The best way to pitch Ruth is to pitch behind him. He has no weaknesses except deliberate walks. You have your choice—one base on four balls or four bases on one ball."
> —Waite Hoyt to Red Lucas

Believing Ruth was a has-been, Lucas and others laughed. By the end of the game, it was the Sultan of Swat who was laughing all the way home. Babe hit his 712th career homer off Red Lucas. Babe's next two came courtesy of Guy Bush, the last one being the homer that would go down in history—number 714.

> "A prodigious clout that carried clear over the right field grandstand, bounded into the street and rolled into Schenley Park."
> —Associated Press

Babe's three home runs that day weren't enough to save the game as the Pirates won 11–7. Nor did they mark an upturn for Babe. Eight days later, on June 2, Babe Ruth turned in his walking papers.

> "I played just a little too long. About a week or so. I should have quit that day in Pittsburgh."
> —Babe Ruth in *The Babe Ruth Story*

In the twenty-eight games Babe played with the Braves, he had twelve RBIs and six home runs. When he retired, his 714 total career homers were more than twice as many home runs as any other MLB player.

After leaving the Braves, the Babe made public appearances, attended charity functions, made speeches, and signed autographs. He golfed, he hunted, he boated, he bowled, and he missed baseball. He especially missed being part of a team.

> "I wanted to stay in baseball more than I ever wanted anything in my life. But in 1935 there was no job for me . . . I felt certain that the phone would ring and it would be the Yankees or some other big-league team in search of me . . . But the phone didn't ring."
> —Babe Ruth in *The Babe Ruth Story*

But Babe's phone did finally ring. In June 1938, Larry MacPhail, now executive vice president of the Brooklyn Dodgers, signed Babe as coach for the remainder of the 1938 season at a salary of $15,000. MacPhail later said he "signed Ruth for his 'inspirational value' to the seventh-place Dodgers" ("Babe Ruth Crossed Paths with the Dodgers as More Than a Coach," Jon Weisman, *Dodger Insider*, September 9, 2014).

"I would have been back long before if I had the chance to hook on with some major league club. But what could I do? I didn't get any offers. You can't make a guy give you a job. When I was offered one I grabbed it quick."
—Babe Ruth in *The Boston Globe*, June 19, 1938

More than twenty-eight thousand fans turned up for Babe's first day of coaching on June 19, 1938. The stadium crackled with excitement over his return. The crowd whooped and cheered Babe's every move.

"Sound the loud trumpet! Or as John Keats put it: 'What pipes and timbrels? What wild ecstasy?' It's Prometheus Unbound, if a title from Shelly may be borrowed for the great occasion."
—John Kiernan, "All the Fun, or the Babe Comes Back," *The New York Times*, June 19, 1938

Babe brought new energy to the dugout too. Except for Leo Durocher, who was against Babe from the start, the players were excited to have him on the team. Outfielder Kiki Cuyler, then in the last season of a long career, noted, "That guy is amazing. He even does something to me" (*Babe: The Legend Comes to Life* by Robert W. Creamer).

Adding "The Great Bambino" to the Dodgers' coaching staff did exactly what MacPhail hoped it would. According to *Baseball Almanac* attendance data, during the Brooklyn Dodgers' 1938 season, nearly 200,000 more fans than the previous year turned up for games, "close to 100,000 more than the National League average that season."

Unfortunately, due in large part due to Leo Durocher's Shakespeare-esque machinations, Babe's hopes of his coaching debut with the Dodgers launching a career in management were dashed.

"Ruth's arrival as a Brooklyn Dodger coach in 1938 seemed, at first glance, to offer him a plausible path to a managerial position and a way to overcome the unfair treatment that Ruth received with the Braves in 1935. But with MacPhail being firmly in Durocher's corner and Durocher being staunchly opposed to Ruth, there is no realistic way to expect that Ruth could ever have been named manager of the Dodgers under that arrangement. Paralleling his time with the Boston Braves, the opportunity to coach the Brooklyn Dodgers was, for Ruth, a case of being in the wrong place at the wrong time. Ruth, it seems, deserved better fortunes."
—John McMurray, "Babe Ruth, Brooklyn Dodgers Coach," *Baseball Research Journal*, fall 2015

By 1946, the Babe's family realized there was something seriously wrong with his health. The Babe, always big and burly—as one reporter put it, "built like a bale of cotton"—was shedding weight—eighty pounds since the previous year. His voice was raspy, and he experienced horrific head pain, especially behind his left eye. In November, Babe was admitted to the hospital for "observation." Although no one told him, and reporters never printed it, the Babe had what is commonly believed to have been throat cancer. That winter, Babe had a throat operation. Afterward, he had increasingly more trouble swallowing and difficulty talking.

Babe Ruth's actual illness was nasopharyngeal cancer, a rare and deadly cancer in the back of the nose and mouth. The cancer produced a large tumor at the base of his skull that pressed on his brain and caused those awful headaches. It was inoperable at the time.

Even while battling a terminal illness, the Babe set records. He volunteered to be among the first cancer patients to receive both radiation and chemotherapy at the same time—a treatment that had yet to be used on humans. And while these treatments couldn't save Babe, the experimental therapies he underwent would become standard cancer treatment.

> "I realized that if anything was learned about that type of treatment, whether good or bad, it would be of use in the future to the medical profession and maybe to a lot of people with my same trouble."
> —Babe Ruth in *The Babe Ruth Story*

Baseball Commissioner Happy Chandler declared Sunday, April 27, 1947, Babe Ruth Day in every major league ballpark. The Babe attended the celebration at Yankee Stadium. He was presented with a silver trophy and a shiny black Lincoln Continental from Ford Motor Company. A thirteen-year-old representing the American Legion Baseball Program introduced him. Dressed in a tan double-breasted suit, impeccable, as always, Babe leaned into the microphone. To listeners, it seemed as though he was addressing the children in the crowd—or the child he was. His voice was faint and raspy as he addressed the 58,339 fans who packed the stadium:

> "The only real game, I think, is baseball. You have to start from way down at the bottom . . . You've got to let it grow up with you. And if you're successful and try hard enough, you're bound to come out on top."

The Babe suited up in his New York Yankees uniform one final time. On June 13, 1948, Yankee Stadium held a celebration commemorating the twenty-fifth anniversary of the opening day game in his ballpark—The House That Ruth Built—and retired his No. 3 jersey for all time. Other members of the 1923 team—Wally Pipp, Joe Dugan, Hinkey Haines, Waite Hoyt, George Pipgras, Joe Bush, Oscar Roettger, Bob Meusel, Elmer Smith, Sam Jones, Wally Schang, Carl Mays, Whitey Witt, Fred Hofmann, and Mike McNally—were there too. New York City Mayor William O'Dwyer welcomed everyone, especially "Babe Ruth, the hero of all our baseball days."

When his name was called, Babe let his topcoat fall. Too sick and frail to stand on his own, using a bat as a cane, he made his way to the microphone. As the crowd rose in a thunderous ovation, Babe smiled and waved. He leaned in to address the crowd:

"I am proud I hit the first home run here in 1923. It was marvelous to see 13 or 14 players who were my teammates going back 25 years. I'm telling you it makes me proud and happy to be here."

By July, Babe was back in the hospital. Fans kept vigil outside Memorial Hospital in New York City (now Memorial Sloan-Kettering Hospital). When he felt up to it, Babe autographed cards and dropped them out the window of his hospital room to the kids on the street.

"If anything could have saved him, believe me, the prayers would have."
—Julia Ruth Stevens

On July 26, Babe left the hospital one last time to attend the premiere of **The Babe Ruth Story**, a fictionalized biography starring actor William Bendix. Babe had coached Bendix for the role. Coincidentally, although not much of an athlete, in 1922, Bendix had been a bat boy at Yankee Stadium. Alas, Babe was so ill, he had to leave the premier before the end of the movie.

George Herman "Babe" Ruth Jr. died shortly after 8 p.m. on August 16, 1948, of complications from nasopharyngeal cancer. He was fifty-three years old. For two days, August 17 and 18, he lay in state at the entrance to Yankee Stadium. An estimated seventy thousand people waited in line for hours to pay their respects. There were eight official pallbearers, including Connie Mack, owner and manager of the Philadelphia Athletics; sportswriter Fred Lieb; and teammates Waite Hoyt, Whitey Whitt, and Joe Dugan, as well as fifty-seven honorary pallbearers. He was laid to rest in the Gate of Heaven Cemetery in Valhalla, New York.

In his twenty-two-season career (1914–35, with the Red Sox, Yankees, and Braves), George Herman Ruth Jr.—Jidge, The Great Bambino, Big Bam, Colossus of Clout, Behemoth of Bust, Mammoth of Maul, Mauling Mastodon, Mauling Monarch, Prince of Pounders, King of Crash, King of Clout, Colossus of Crash, King of Swing, Sultan of Swat, Terrible Titan, Kid of Crash, Blunderbuss, The Babe—led both the American League and National League in slugging percentage and OPS thirteen times, home runs twelve times, and walks eleven times. He also led in runs scored eight times, RBI five times, and slugged at least .700 in nine seasons. He stole 123 bases, including stealing home ten times! When he retired in 1935, he held fifty-six MLB records, some of which still stand. And twice, in 1918 and 1919, he hit ten home runs as a batter and made thirty strikeouts as a pitcher, a two-way record that stood for the next one hundred years. It was not until 2018 that Angels' pitcher Shohei Ohtani matched him.

Speaking of standing records, hard as they try, at the time of publication, there's yet to come an MLB player in modern baseball who can beat the Babe's Single Season Runs Scored record of 177 or Extra-Base Hits (XBH) record of 119, Career On Base Plus Slugging (OPS) record of 1.164 and OPS+ of 206, or his Total Base (TB) record of 457, set in 1921.

Babe Ruth remains the benchmark against which other players are measured. In 1949, a year after his death, the first Babe Ruth Award, honoring the World Series MVP, was given to New York Yankee pitcher Joe Page. Modified in 2003, the award now honors the player with the best postseason performance. Sandy Koufax and Jack Morris each won the award twice. Adolis Garcia received it in 2023.

The Babe Ruth Home Run Award, sponsored by Sullivan Artworks, recognizing the previous season's leading MLB home run hitter, was first awarded in 1998. The twenty-one-pound (9.5 kilograms), twenty-inch-high (51 centimeters) bronze statue of Ruth, modeled after a 1920 photograph of him following through on a tremendous swing, was given to Mark McGwire. Alex Rodriguez won it three times. Other recipients include Jim Thome, Sammy Sosa, and Ryan Howard (twice). Albert Pujols was the last recipient in 2009.

And visually most impressive of all—because it's actually fit for royalty—is the Babe Ruth Sultan of Swat Crown, honoring MLB's top slugger. The first crown was awarded in 1956 to Mickey Mantle, and Willie Mays was crowned twice, in 1962 and 1965. Sadaharu Oh, in 1985, was the last recipient until 2024, when the Babe Ruth Museum revived the tradition. On May 1, 2024, in a ceremony at Camden Yard, Yankees slugger Aaron Judge was crowned.

Babe's legacy lives on with these awards, as well as through children, where he'd want it to most. Since 1951, the Babe Ruth League, an international youth baseball and softball league, has been supporting and developing baseball players. The League, which has expanded to five divisions for boys and girls ages four to eighteen, is where many Hall of Famers got their start, including Carl Yastrzemski, Joe Morgan, Jim Palmer, Rod Carew, George Brett, Nolan Ryan, Cal Ripken Jr., Frank Thomas, Randy Johnson, John Smoltz, and Mike Piazza.

On November 16, 2018, Babe Ruth was posthumously awarded the Presidential Medal of Freedom. It is the nation's highest civilian honor.

"BASEBALL IS THE GREATEST GAME IN THE WORLD AND DESERVES THE BEST YOU CAN GIVE IT."

Babe tips his cap to fans. Yankees' dugout, circa 1927.

BABE RUTH CAREER BATTING STATS

Major League Games	2,503
Minor League Games	46
At-Bats (AB)	8,399
Bases on Balls (BB)	2,062
Hits	2,873
Total Bases	7,972
Runs Scored	2,174
Steals (SB)	123
Lifetime BA	.342
Home Run Average	11.8
Slugging Percentage	.690
On-Base Percentage for Right Fielder (OBP)	.474
Runs Batted In (RBI)	2,214
Multi-Homer Games	72
Career Singles (1B)	1,517
Career Doubles (2B)	506
Career Triples (3B)	136
Career Homers (HR)	714*

+MAKE THAT A BIG 715!

In the July 8, 1918, game against the Cleveland Indians, bottom of the tenth inning, with the score tied 0–0 and Amos Struck on first, Babe blasted a homer into Fenway Park's right field stands. Because, as Struck touched home plate to score the winning run, the game was technically over, Babe was credited with an RBI and a triple but not a home run.

Record keeping in early MLB records—even home run stats—weren't such a big deal in those days. In the 1960s, however, baseball historian David Neft set out to set the records straight. In his book *Lore of the Bambino*, Jonathan Weeks noted that Neft and his team of researchers unearthed, among other discrepancies, thirty-seven unrecorded homers, including what would have been Babe's 715th career home run. The MLB assembled a special committee to determine how to deal with the findings. They unanimously agreed to credit the home runs to all thirty-seven players.

But get this: Records for the thirty-six other runs were adjusted accordingly, but not Babe Ruth's. Why? Because by then, as sportswriter Joe Posnanski noted, Babe's record-setting 714 was a number "every red-blooded American fan knew by heart." At the urging of a committee member who'd been absent when the vote was taken, another vote was taken. The final count was 3–2 in favor of leaving Babe Ruth's record at 714.

"With vim and verve, he has walloped the curve from Texas to Duluth;
Which is no small task, and I beg to ask: Was there ever a guy like Ruth?"
—excerpted from "A Query (Was There Ever A Guy Like Ruth?)" by John Kieran, published in *The New York Times* on October 1, 1927, after Babe Ruth hit his record-setting sixtieth home run of the season

"NEVER LET THE FEAR OF STRIKING OUT GET IN YOUR WAY."

"Life had a way of regularly knocking Babe Ruth down. But, he always got up,
and, when he did, he swung for the fences. Americans, everywhere, loved him for it."
—Bill Jenkinson

"April Fools" Babe taking a whack at a huge baseball, April 1, 1927, in Jacksonville, Florida. Babe Ruth's lifetime strike-out total was 1330, an MLB record that stood until another mega-hitter, "Mr. October," broke it. Reggie Jackson's career strike-out record of 2,597 still stands.

BIBLIOGRAPHY

There are scores of books about Babe Ruth for readers of all levels. Most are available from a library. Below are some we found especially interesting and helpful in providing a better understanding of baseball, The Babe, and the times. *Happy reading!*

BOOKS WRITTEN BY GEORGE HERMAN "BABE" RUTH (WITH AND/OR BY GHOST WRITERS)
Babe Ruth's Big Book of Baseball by George Herman Ruth, 1935 edition.
Babe Ruth's Own Book of Baseball by George Herman Ruth, 1928. Reprinted by the University of Nebraska Press, 1992.
How to Play Baseball by Babe Ruth, 1931.
The Babe Ruth Story by Babe Ruth (as told to Bob Considine), 1948.
Playing the Game: My Early Years in Baseball by Babe Ruth, edited by William R. Cobb, 2011. Babe's autobiography, mostly ghost written, published in newspaper serializations during the 1920 baseball season.

PICTURE BOOKS
Home Run: The Story of Babe Ruth by Robert Burleigh, illustrated by Mike Wimmer, 1998. Biography of Babe Ruth told in brief, powerful narrative and "bubble gum trading card"–style factoid bites.
Becoming Babe Ruth by Matt Tavares, 2013. Story of Babe Ruth's boyhood in St. Mary's, Brother Mathias's big hits, and how, after a fire destroyed the school, Babe helped raise funds to rebuild the school by having the St. Mary's band join the Yankees on tour.

GRAPHIC COMIC-STYLE
Babe Ruth: Baseball's All-Time Best by James Buckley Jr., illustrated by Kelly Tindall, 2020. A graphic biography—comic book style—part of the Show Me History series. Two kid characters, Sam and Libby, at a baseball game talking about Babe Ruth, beginning with the April 18, 1923, opening day game in Yankee Stadium.

CHAPTER BOOKS
The Story of Babe Ruth: Baseball's Greatest Legend by Lisa Eisenberg, 1997. Famous Lives series. A comprehensive, easy-to-read biography with photographs.
Babe Ruth and the Ice Cream Mess by Dan Gutman, illustrated by Elaine Garvin, 2004. A level two book in the Ready-to-Read series.
Who Was Babe Ruth? by Joan Holub, illustrated by Ted Hammond, 2012. Excellent biography; twelve chapters, 102 pages plus bibliography for second to fourth grade.
Babe Ruth and the Baseball Curse by David A. Kelly, illustrated by Tim Jessell, 2009. Part of the Totally True Adventures series, this is the novelized story of how Babe Ruth "cursed" the Red Sox to how and when the curse was broken.
Babe Ruth by Norman L. Macht, 1991. Part of the Baseball Legends series, sixty-four pages, brief chapters with photographs highlighting phases of Babe's life. Life chronology and Babe's baseball stats in back.
Babe Ruth by Don McLeese, 2003. Beginning reader, twenty-four pages with photographs.
Babe Ruth: The Big Moments of the Big Fella by Tom Meany, 1947. A biography for young readers with a few photographs.
Babe Ruth: Sultan of Swat by Lois P. Nicholson, 1994. Middle grade biography with illustrations.

ADULT BOOKS

Fifty-Nine in '84: Old Hoss Radbourn, Barehanded Baseball, and the Greatest Season a Pitcher Ever Had by Edward Achorn, 2010. Charles Radbourn was a major league pitcher who won fifty-nine games in 1884. This is an excellent book for anyone wanting to learn about early baseball.

Babe: The Legend Comes to Life by Robert Creamer, 1992. An excellent, easy-to-read biography with lots of pictures.

Hank Greenberg: The Story of My Life by Hank Greenberg with Ira Kerkow, 1969. Greenberg's biography in which he talks about other players, including Babe Ruth.

The Big Fella: Babe Ruth and the World He Created by Jane Leavy, 2018. Great readability! Over six hundred pages centered around Babe Ruth and Lou Gehrig's twenty-one-day barnstorming tour in 1927.

Babe Ruth: A Twentieth-Century Life by Wilborn Hampton, 2009. Easy-to-read "light" biography—bigger print. Lots of "direct" quotes with sources listed in the back.

Babe Ruth: Against All Odds, World's Mightiest Slugger by Bill Jenkinson, 2014. Jenkinson, the undisputed leading Ruthian scholar, condensed thirty-five years of research on Babe into this biography, chronicling who Babe really was and what he accomplished.

Baseball's Ultimate Power: Ranking the All-Time Greatest Distance Home Run Hitters by Bill Jenkinson, 2010. "Tape-measure home run" nerds, this is for you! Babe, Robinson, Foxx, Mays, Mantle, Gibson—featuring photos, diagrams, and detailed descriptions of baseball's longest homers and long balls hit by the mightiest hitters in major league history—including long-ball hitters from the Negro Leagues.

The Year Babe Ruth Hit 104: Home Runs: Recrowning Baseball's Greatest Slugger by Bill Jenkinson, 2007. If you want to know about every home run and long ball fly Babe Ruth ever hit—along with statistical information—this is a fascinating read. Jenkinson maintains, with supporting data, that under modern rules, the Babe would have hit 104 homers in 1921, ninety in other seasons, and over sixty several times.

The Man Who Made Babe Ruth: Brother Matthias of St. Mary's School by Brian Martin, 2020. A thoroughly researched biography of Babe's mentor, Brother Matthias, the Xaverian Brothers, and St. Mary's Industrial School.

The Babe Book: Baseball's Greatest Legend Remembered by Ernestine Miller, 2000. With a forward by Julia Ruth Stevens. A book of quotes using photos from the Babe Ruth Birthplace and Orioles Museum in Baltimore.

The Big Bam: The Life and Times of Babe Ruth by Leigh Montville, 2006. Reads like a novel. Montville sifted through other Babe Ruth biographies, interviews with him and other players, and other writer's notes to put together a story that is an enjoyable read and at the same time compares and contrasts the disparate stories about Babe Ruth and his life.

My Dad, the Babe: Growing Up with an American Hero by Dorothy Ruth Pirone with Chris Martens, 1988. An autobiography/biography of Babe Ruth as told by his daughter Dorothy. A different perspective than most.

The Tumult and the Shouting: My Life in Sports by Grantland Rice, 1954. Sportswriter Grantland Rice's memoire, including stories about sports and athletes of all sorts from the first half of the twentieth century. Rice's writing is a joy to read!

The Glory of Their Times: The Story of the Early Days of Baseball Told by the Men Who Played it by Lawrence S. Ritter, 1966. Fascinating interviews with ball players talking about other ball players.

The Babe: A Life in Pictures by Laurence S. Ritter and Mark Rucker, 1988. An oversized coffee table–style photo-biography told in caption bites—280 pages with about that many photos.

Babe Ruth: Remembering the Bambino in Stories, Photos, and Memorabilia by Julia Ruth Stevens and Bill Gilbert, 2008. A biography of Babe written by his daughter Julia. Great photos and sleeves with interesting reproductions of contracts, tickets, programs, and quotes from players.

Yankees Century: 100 Years of New York Yankees Baseball by Glenn Stout and Richard A. Johnson, 2002. A coffee-table style book with 250-some photographs and brief essays on players and the history of the team.

Lore of the Bambino: 100 Great Babe Ruth Stories by Jonathan Weeks, 2022. Great stories and excellent back matter, including records set, movies made, products endorsed, and salaries earned.

Babe Ruth and the 1918 Red Sox: Babe Ruth and the World Champion Boston Red Sox by Allan Wood, 2000. Wood's extensive research and lively narrative brings to life a time when the Red Sox ruled the American League. In addition to poring over miles of microfilm, Wood spoke with descendants of the 1918 players, as well as two men who knew Babe Ruth in 1918. The book includes thirty-four pages of photographs.

ACKNOWLEDGMENTS

Out of the Mouth of Babe, as the title says, is all about Babe—what he said—so first, our gratitude and appreciation goes out to the sportswriters who recorded and reported Babe Ruth's words and feats in such vivid, colorful language that it still begs to be read, as well as to the news services that published them. *Newspapers rock!* It is through their efforts that we have stories and game accounts, along with newsreels and movies by which we "know" Babe. That those accounts are available today is due to the herculean (dare I write "Ruthian") efforts of baseball fans, biographers, STATS "nerds/geeks," and historians, including members of the Society for American Baseball Research (SABR); the Babe Ruth Birthplace Museum; the Negro Leagues Baseball Museum; John Horne and Cassidy Lent at the National Baseball Hall of Fame; NY Yankees Museum Curator Brian Richards; Library of Congress Reference Librarian Joanna Colclough; Hot Springs biggest fans, Derek Phillips, Steve Arrison and Susan Dugan; the folks at Westhampton Free Library; and librarians everywhere—three cheers for interlibrary loan!

There is no "I" in "baseball" or "books." This book exists thanks to all the people who helped bring it together, especially the team at Familius who said "Yes!" As for any mistakes, those are on me/us. Last and most, huge thanks to Tim Reid, Bill Jenkinson, Marty Appel, Larry Hogan, and the Ruth Stevens family (especially Babe's grandson, Tom Stevens), who—from conception to actualization—served as resources, readers, and cheerleaders.

PHOTO CREDITS

Babe Ruth bequeathed his belongings, including uniforms, bats, baseballs, equipment and memorabilia to the National Baseball Hall of Fame and Museum in Cooperstown, New York. Some of those items are on display in the Babe Ruth Room in the Museum. Many of these photos are reprinted from copies in the Ruth-Stevens Family Collection. Due diligence was given to sourcing; photos reprinted herein are either deemed to be in the public domain or used with permission as noted.

Cover: Babe Hecking Opposing Team
National Baseball Hall of Fame and Museum, Cooperstown, N.Y.
1. Babe Ruth Signature Swing (signed)
Ruth-Stevens Family Collection
2. Babe Ruth on Car with Kids
National Baseball Hall of Fame and Museum, Cooperstown, N.Y.
3. Babe Surely Babe HR With Catcher and Umpire
Courtesy of the Boston Public Library, Leslie Jones Collection
4. Ruth Gehrig Fresno Japanese American Players
National Baseball Hall of Fame and Museum, Cooperstown, N.Y.
5. Babe Teenager Outfield
Babe Ruth Birthplace Museum
6. Babe Sparring with Artie Johnson

National Baseball Hall of FAme and Museum, Cooperstown,N.Y.
7. BR with Red Sox Players
Bain Collection / Library of Congress
8. Babe Ruth Outfield Going Back for Catch
National Baseball Hall of Fame and Museum, Cooperstown, N.Y.
9. "Josh and The Babe"
Painting by Bill Purdom courtesy of his estate.
10. Babe Ruth Anna Nilsson Movie Still
National Baseball Hall of Fame and Museum, Cooperstown, N.Y.
11. Peerless Babe Ruth
Underwood & Underwood / Library of Congress
12. Providence Grays with Babe Ruth
General Photo Co, Providence, RI / Wikimedia

13. Babe Ruth with Boys as They Slide at Plate
Ruth-Stevens Family Collection
14. Foxx Ruth Gehrig Simmons
Creative Commons / Wikimedia (must show link to this attribution: https://creativecommons.org/licenses/by/1.0/deed.en)
15. Babe Ruth with Log at Home Plate Farm
National Photo Company Collection / Library of Congress
16. 2 Images: Yankee Stadium April 18, 1923
Yankee Stadium First Opening Day; National Baseball Hall of Fame and Museum, Cooperstown, N.Y. / MLB.com
Yankees on Field 1923; Library of Congress
17. Gehrig Ruth Rodeo
National Baseball Hall of Fame and Museum, Cooperstown, N.Y.
18. Babe Ruth with Brooklyn Royal Giants Catcher
Unknown
19. Babe Ruth's 1921 Barnstorming Tour Promotional Card
Rucker Archive / Society of American Baseball Research
20. BR at Wells Motors
St. Louis Post-Dispatch
21. Babe Pitching Majestic Park
Courtesy of Garland County Historical Society
22. Babe and Claire with Kids at Beach
Ruth-Stevens Family Collection
23. Babe Ruth Knocked Out
National Photo Company Collection / Library of Congress
24. 4 images: BR Product Labels
Ruth's Home Run Candy Bar; George H Ruth Candy Company, 1926.
BR Red Rock Cola; The Red Rock Company
BR Juniors Underwear; Sealpax. Rubin Metzler Company.
Babe Ruth Big League Chewing Gum 1933; Library of Congress
25. Babe Ruth Sliding into Home Plate
National Baseball Hall of Fame and Museum, Cooperstown, N.Y.
26. Babe Ruth on Bike in Baltimore 1914
Charles Colon
27. 1927 Yankees (Murderers Row)
Cosmo News Photo Service

28. Babe Ruth in Military Uniform
National Photo Company Collection / Library of Congress
29. Babe Ruth, Lou Gehrig and Others
Rucker Archive / Society of American Baseball Research
30. Babe Ruth with Trainer
Ruth-Stevens Family Collection
31. 2 images: Dunsmuir
Babe Ruth at Bat Dunsmuir Oct 24: Paul Standar / California State University, Chico, Meriam Library
Special Collections
Babe Ruth Mt. Shasta Girl's Team 10-19-24: Courtesy of Siskiyou County Yreka, CA.
32. Babe Ruth and Shoeless Joe Jackson
NY Daily News / Wikimedia Commons
33. Babe in Batting Stance with Catcher and Umpire
Rucker Archive / Society for American Baseball Research
34. BR Pointing Called Shot
Still from 16mm movie taken by Matt Kandle Sr.
35. Ruth and Jack Dempsey with Big Bat
Rucker Archive / Society of American Baseball Research
36. 4 images: Collage of Cartoons
Caricature of Babe; Miguel Covarrubias / Library of Congress
Babe 21st Season; Ruth-Steven Family Collection
Babe Hot Springs Cartoon; Boston Post, Mar 23, 1918.
Babe Wash Times Cartoon; Washing Times, Jan 8, 1920 "Chronicling America Collection" / Library of
Congress
37. Babe and Waite Hoyte
National Baseball Hall of Fame and Museum, Cooperstown, N.Y.
38. 3 images: Scientific Tests
Ruth Hitting Article; Richmond Times-Dispatch, July 18, 1920 / "Chronicling America Collection" / Library
of Congress
Babe Ruth Tests; Popular Science Monthly, Oct 1921.
Babe Ruth Test Swing; Popular Science Monthly, Oct 1921.
39. Babe Ruth Celebrating Home Ruth with Family
Ruth-Stevens Family Collection
40. 2 images: Japan Tour
Babe with US Players on Japan Tour; Ruth-Stevens Family Collection
Babe with Japanese Umbrella; Everett Collection

41. 3 images: Progression of Golf Swing
Ruth with Golf Clubs; Ruth-Stevens Family Collection
Ruth in Back Golf Swing; Ruth-Stevens Family Collection
Ruth Follow Through; Ruth-Stevens Family Collection
42. Babe with Dog in Park
Photo taken by Hazel the dog's owner; name unknown / Chicago Sun-Times Aug 20. 2015.
43. The Babe Bows Out
Nat Fein / NY Herald Tribune / Wikimedia Commons
44. Babe Ruth Signing Baseballs
National Baseball Hall of Fame and Museum, Cooperstown, N.Y.
45. Babe Ruth and Ty Cobb 1920
Christy Walsh & International Newsreel / Library of Congress
46. 8 images: Funeral (1) & Telegram Collage (7)
Fans Line Up at Babe Viewing Yankee Stadium; Rucker Archive / Society of American Baseball Research
Western Union Telegrams; Ruth Stevens Family Collection
47. Babe Ruth St. Mary's Baseball Team
Sporting News Collection / Wikimedia Commons
48. Ruth Sliding into Base-Still
First National / Ruth-Stevens Family Collection
49. 2 images: BR and Johnny Sylvester; Courtesy of Andrew Lilley / Loose Gravel Films
BR Letter to Young Johnny Sylvester ; Courtesy of Andrew Lilley / Loose Gravel Films
50. Babe Bats in Boston
Rucker Archive / Society of American Baseball Research
51. Babe Wally Berger Hal Lee 1935
Courtesy of the Boston Public Library, Leslie Jones Collection
52. Babe Ruth with Baseball Legion Boy
Ruth-Stevens Family Collection
53. Hall of Fame Members June 12 1939
National Baseball Hall of Fame and Museum, Cooperstown, N.Y.
54. Babe Ruth Diving into Pool
National Baseball Hall of Fame and Museum, Cooperstown, N.Y.
55. Babe Ruth and Herbert Hoover 1933
U.S. National Archives and Records Administration
56. 2 images: Babe Ruth Pitching
Babe Ruth Pitching for New York; Bain Collection / Library of Congress
Prouder of My Pitching ; Kelly Bennett / Babe Ruth Exhibit NBHF

57. Brother Matthias with Babe
Xaverian Brothers USA
58. Ruth Batting Huge Fake Ball
Ruth-Stevens Family Collection
59. Babe Ruth Tipping His Cap
Rucker Archive / Society of American Baseball Research

Poems:
"Sultan of Swat" by John Lardner, originally published in Franklin Pierce Adams (F.P.A.) syndicated column,
"The Conning Tower," reprinted by permission of Susan Lardner.
"R is for Ruth...Just R is for Ruth" excerpt from "Line Up For Yesterday" by Ogden Nash.
Copyright © 1935 by Ogden Nash, renewed. Reprinted by permission of Curtis Brown, Ltd.

Ruthian efforts were made to correctly source photographs, excerpts, and quotations, as well as to secure permissions, when needed. If there are any mistakes or omissions, please bring it to our attention so the publisher can correct it in the next printing.

"To say 'Babe Ruth' is to say 'Baseball.'"
—Will Harridge, President of the American League, 1931–59

ABOUT THE AUTHORS

KELLY BENNETT

comes from a family of baseball fan-a-tics! She is the author of many award-winning books for children—mostly picture books– including *The House that Ruth Built* a non-fiction lyrical account of the opening day game in Yankee Stadium and the Babe's big wish, illustrated by Susanna Covelli, also published by Familius. Her stories, such as *Not Norman, A Goldfish Story and Norman, One Amazing Goldfish; Vampire Baby; Your Daddy Was Just Like You; Dance, Y'all, Dance; Dad and Pop; and One Day I Went Rambling*, celebrate imagination, families, friends, pets . . . all that goes into being a kid! She divides her time between Houston, TX, Westhampton Beach, NY, and Mimiville (which is anywhere her grandboys may be.)

To see more, please visit www.kellybennett.com.

BRENT STEVENS

is the great-grandson of Babe Ruth and he has made it part of his life's mission to ensure a positive, lasting legacy for his great grandfather.   Brent is a collector of baseball cards and owns some unique pieces of Babe Ruth memorabilia. Loving his family history, he treasured spending much time with his grandmother, Julia Ruth Stevens, Babe's daughter, until she passed away in March 2019 at the age of 101.

He is happily married to Marie and the proud father to two wonderful girls, Lexi and Maddy. They along with their golden doodle, Cooper, call Roswell, GA home. Originally born in Concord, NH, Brent spent his early years living in New England, Saudi Arabia, as well as upstate New York before putting down roots in the Atlanta area. Brent is passionate about travelling and makes it a point to get overseas at least once a year with his family. He has an undergraduate degree in Finance from Binghamton University in New York, as well as an MBA from the University of Georgia. Brent has spent most of his career supporting project delivery and operations at Cox Enterprises.

In addition to his primary job at Cox, Brent is also an avid entrepreneur engaged in several business projects, including BR3 Enterprises, LLC, which he co-owns with long-time business partner and friend, Stu Dressler. He is co-creator of the Babe Ruth tribute site, BabeRuthCentral.com, which receives continued praise and engagement from Babe Ruth and general Baseball fans of all ages. Through his shared company, BR Goods, he has co-developed multiple Babe Ruth-related products, including a wide range of Babe-related artwork and apparel, as well as "Babe Ruth's Family Kitchen" – a line of condiments inspired by Babe's own recipes. Brent attends many events and participates in many interviews representing the Family of Babe Ruth.

STU DRESSLER

comes to the Babe Ruth world through his long personal and professional relationship with the Family of Babe Ruth (the Ruth-Stevens family), particularly Babe's great-grandson Brent Stevens. Stu and Brent co-wrote and co-developed BabeRuthCentral.com which has been engaging Babe Ruth fans and others worldwide since 2006. Stu and Brent also partnered with Sean Gibson, Josh Gibson's great-grandson, to commission a "what if they met" painting of Babe and Josh which was featured in the New York Times.

Stu grew up just outside of Pittsburgh, PA and went on to earn a BS in Finance at Penn State and an MBA from the University of Michigan. Stu's professional experiences included 15-years at General Motors. In addition to starting up and developing GM's first online ownership loyalty portal worldwide, Stu served as the brand planner for HUMMER. Many of his roles at GM required extensive international travel and Stu was fortunate to work on the ground in 18 countries and reside in Zurich, Switzerland for a time. After GM, Stu went on to many consulting roles, but eventually became a founder of a business for Cox Automotive in Atlanta, GA, where he and his co-founders grew that business from a blank sheet of paper to a $150 million business in 8 years.

In 2022, Stu retired quite early from his corporate and professional to focus on his biggest passion – travel – and started a successful travel business as a result. That business is quite active today, designing trips all over the world and helping people learn and grow through travel. Stu intends to write a series of children's books based on his own travel experiences which so far include 49 of 50 states, 71 countries and 6 continents. Stu currently resides in Atlanta, GA with his beloved "co-pilot", Dune, the Dingo dog.

ABOUT FAMILIUS

VISIT OUR WEBSITE: WWW.FAMILIUS.COM

Familius is a global trade publishing company that publishes books and other content to help families be happy. We believe that happy families are key to a better society and the foundation of a happy life. The greatest work anyone will ever do will be within the walls of his or her own home. And we don't mean vacuuming! We recognize that every family looks different and passionately believe in helping all families find greater joy, whatever their situation. To that end, we publish beautiful books that help families live our 10 Habits of Happy Family Life: *love together, play together, learn together, work together, talk together, heal together, read together, eat together, give together*, and *laugh together*. Further, Familius does not discriminate on the basis of race, color, religion, gender, age, nationality, disability, caste, or sexual orientation in any of its activities or operations. Founded in 2012, Familius is located in Sanger, California.

CONNECT

Facebook: www.facebook.com/familiusbooks
Pinterest: www.pinterest.com/familiusbooks
Instagram: @FamiliusBooks
TikTok: @FamiliusBooks

FAMILIUS

THE MOST IMPORTANT WORK YOU EVER DO WILL BE WITHIN THE WALLS OF YOUR OWN HOME.